"WE SHALL NEVER SURRENDER!"

"The Battle of France is over. The Battle of Britain is about to begin. . . . The whole fury and might of the enemy must very soon be turned on us. Hitler knows that he will have to break us in the island or lose the war. . . .

"You ask, what is our policy? I will say; it is to wage war by sea, land and air . . . to wage war against a monstrous tyranny never surpassed in the dark lamentable catalogue of human crime. . . . You ask, what is our aim? I can answer in one word: Victory. . .

"We shall fight on the seas and oceans, we shall fight with growing confidence and growing strength in the air; we shall defend our island, whatever the cost may be. We shall fight on the beaches, we shall fight on the landing-grounds, we shall fight in the fields and in the streets, we shall fight in the hills; we shall never surrender. . ."

THE BANTAM WAR BOOK SERIES

This is a series of books about a world on fire.

These carefully chosen volumes cover the full dramatic sweep of World War II. Many are eyewitness accounts by the men who fought in this global conflict in which the future of the civilized world hung in balance. Fighter pilots, tank commanders and infantry commanders, among others, recount exploits of individual courage in the midst of the large-scale terrors of war. They present portraits of brave men and true stories of gallantry and cowardice in action, moving sagas of survival and tragedies of untimely death. Some of the stories are told from the enemy viewpoint to give the reader an immediate sense of the incredible life and death struggle of both sides of the battle.

Through these books we begin to discover what it was like to be there, a participant in an epic war for freedom.

Each of the books in the Bantam War Book series contains a dramatic color painting and illustrations specially commissioned for each title to give the reader a deeper understanding of the roles played by the men and machines of World War II.

CHURCHILL AND THE GENERALS

BY BARRIE PITT

EDITORIAL CONSULTANT JACK LE VIEN

An account of the events
upon which the BBC-Le Vien TV play
by Ian Curteis,
CHURCHILL AND THE GENERALS,
was based.

BANTAM BOOKS
TORONTO · NEW YORK · LONDON

CHURCHILL AND THE GENERALS
A Giniger Book published by the
K. S. Giniger Company, Inc., New York.
A Bantam Book | March 1981

*Drawings by Tom Beecham, Greg Beecham and Stephen Bach.
Maps by Alan McKnight.*

ISBN 0–553–14610–6

Published simultaneously in the United States and Canada

PRINTED IN THE UNITED STATES OF AMERICA

0 9 8 7 6 5 4 3 2 1

FOREWORD

This book had its genesis in the autumn of 1976 when Cedric Messina, a senior television producer at the BBC, conceived the unique idea of a TV drama based on the fascinating relationships between Winston Churchill and the British and American Generals of World War II. The BBC invited me to act as co-producer because, although an American, I had produced a number of films, television series and TV specials based on Sir Winston's writings with his direct consent and encouragement.

Ian Curteis, one of Britain's foremost television dramatists, was assigned to prepare the screenplay. Alan Gibson, a Canadian, brought his considerable experience to bear on the complex task of direction. We were especially fortunate that the BBC appointed as their producer Alan Shallcross, a talented TV veteran. His was the mammoth task of marshalling and deploying a team at times over 300 strong.

After 3 years of intense effort, the program was first televised on the BBC in September 1979 to great critical and public acclaim. At this writing, it is being sponsored on U.S. commercial television by Mobil on the Mobil Showcase Network and is being telecast world-wide in English and foreign-language versions.

With a cast of 16 principal actors, led by Timothy West as Churchill, the program runs almost 3 hours—at the time of its making, the longest single television play ever presented.

Because television is such a transitory medium and because of the success of the program, we commissioned Barrie Pitt, whose chronicling of historic events has brought excitement and enlightenment to millions, to prepare this book based on the same theme.

THE THEME

On 10th May, 1940, when Winston Churchill became Prime Minister and took over control of Britain's war effort, he inherited few practical military plans, little strategy, a strained exchequer, some untried generals, and a German offensive that would soon isolate his country. His first grim duty was to preside over the greatest British defeat in history and it seemed impossible that he could stop the victorious German army from sweeping across the Channel and overwhelming his beloved, beleaguered island.

During a year of mortal peril while England stood alone, he appointed key men to the command of the forces upon which the Free World's survival depended. Men like Wavell, Auchinleck, Slim, Montgomery, Alanbrooke, Alexander, were raised to the highest command, with Churchill himself as Generalissimo—"to wage war," as he said, "against a monstrous tyranny never surpassed in the dark, lamentable catalogue of human crime."

This is the story of his relationships with these remarkable men and the American Generals who followed them. Goading them, driving, bullying and inspiring them, he stood behind them, ordering, whipping, urging on; sometimes impossible, totally ignoring convenient facts, at other times brilliant or cunning, his was the force, which through them began to stem the German tide.

With his personal relish for action he would appear in the field in the strangest uniforms, urging strategies upon his generals which were as likely to be impractical as to be brilliant. With the certain knowledge that only with himself at the helm could Britain win the war, he could ruthlessly sack Wavell or Auchinleck and ride the storm which followed.

It is the story of an erratic, impossible, very English, instinctive genius, pitted against the superb craftmanship of his generals; a story as full of rich humor as it is of cataclysmic events. The focus of this human drama is the sometimes conflicting, sometimes harmonious relations that influenced the destiny of mankind in the supreme crisis of its life.

Although the turning point in the struggle was Russia's entry into the war, not until the might and fury of the United States made itself felt, as "the united, irresistible forces of outraged civilization came to bear upon the criminal," did victory become certain.

From the moment such giants as George Marshall and Dwight Eisenhower appeared on the world stage, the pattern of command changed. Between the Allied Generals and Churchill—himself half American, as he was so fond of pointing out—an entirely new and less intense relationship developed, based on mutual respect and affection. This Grand Alliance, fighting in defense of all that is sacred to man, saved the world from the pestilence of Nazi barbarianism and laid the foundations of Anglo-American unity on which the survival of the Free World depended.

London: *Jack Le Vien*

January 1981

PROLOGUE
MAY 7, 1940

The House of Commons was packed. The mood of the members was frustrated and angry, and although the debate on the war situation had been called by the Labour opposition, some of the most virulent attacks on the government came from its own Conservative supporters. Even the first lord of the admiralty, Mr. Winston Churchill, could not entirely escape censure since he had been largely responsible for sending British and French troops into Norway, where they had suffered the succession of defeats that had precipitated the present angry meeting.

But the sense of outrage in the House stemmed from a source going much farther back than the recent Norwegian failures, and the main force of its anger was pointed directly at the prime minister, Mr. Neville Chamberlain, who now sat just a few places away, pale with anger and humiliation as he listened to the vituperation of which he was clearly the target.

Despite the vast differences in their respective attitudes over the past years and the deeply divisive arguments that had resulted, Mr. Churchill could not avoid a sense of sympathy for his harassed leader. He could hardly remember such bitter personal attacks being mounted in the House of Commons: attacks against the policies of appeasement to which the government had clung for many crucial months; attacks against the pathetic optimism exhibited by the prime minister both in his dealings with Hitler before the war and in his attitude to Britain's ability to defend herself since its outbreak; and most particularly, attacks against the content of a speech Mr. Chamberlain had made only a month before, which had included the unfortunate statement that he believed Hitler had "missed the bus"!

Somehow this remark typified the deliberately blind complacency that characterized Chamberlain, and it had finally roused the House to fury.

There came a brief interlude when Mr. Churchill was able to do a little to protect his baited superior. Sir Roger Keyes rose to castigate the War Cabinet for sending the Royal Navy into action in the North Sea against opposition that was unexpected in both power and position. But Sir Roger was an old friend of Churchill's, and when the first lord made it plain that he was determined to shoulder as much of the blame for this as he could, the force of the admiral's argument waned.

But with Sir Roger back in his seat, the personal attack on Chamberlain rose in crescendo until it reached its zenith with a speech from one of his oldest friends and political colleagues, Mr. Leo Amery. After referring to the need for a political and military fighting spirit to match that of the enemy, Mr. Amery quoted Cromwell's scathing indictment of the leadership of Hamden's army as "old, decaying serving men."

Then, turning directly on the prime minister, he quoted from the Great Protector for the second time: " 'You have sat here too long for any good you have been doing. Depart, I say, and let us have done with you. In the name of God, go!' "

This veritable bombshell served to clarify the mind of the House, and when the debate was resumed the following morning, the Labour opposition announced that they wished it to be treated as a vote of censure on the government. This, Mr. Chamberlain expected, would band the Conservatives together, and he took advantage of this possibility by calling upon "his friends" to support him and his government. This call brought Mr. Lloyd George—prime minister during the previous war—hurrying to the House, but not in response to Mr. Chamberlain's plea. With fine Welsh rhetoric he lambasted the government for its ineffectiveness, its leisureliness, and its inefficiency. When Mr. Churchill intervened to deflect some of the fire from his leader's head, his old mentor warned him sharply that for both his own and the country's good, he must not allow himself to be converted into an air-raid shelter to keep the splinters from hitting his colleagues.

"It is not a question of who are the prime minister's friends," Lloyd George thundered. "It is a far bigger issue. ... He has appealed for sacrifice. The nation is prepared for every sacrifice so long as it has leadership, so long as the government show clearly what they are aiming at, and so long as the nation is confident that those who are leading it are doing their best. I say solemnly that the prime minister should give an example of sacrifice because there is nothing which can contribute more to victory in this war than that he should sacrifice the seals of office."

This was a shrewd blow at Mr. Chamberlain and indeed the entire Cabinet, but they were for the moment buoyed up by the fact that it had been agreed that Mr. Churchill would wind up the debate for them; and in emergency his oratory could be relied upon to swing the balance. But even this comfort was soon to be eroded, for Duff Cooper, who had resigned from Chamberlain's government at the time of Munich, uttered words of warning to the House against just that possibility. "Mr. Churchill," he said, "will be defending with his eloquence those who have so long refused to listen to his counsel, who treated his warnings with contempt and who refused to take him into their own confidence. . . . Those who so often trembled before his sword will be only too glad to shrink behind his buckler. I will beseech my fellow members not to allow the charm of his eloquence and the power of his personality to carry them away tonight. . . ."

And during Churchill's closing speech, it did seem as though the House were accepting Duff Cooper's advice, for the first lord was given a rough time, indeed.

But the government's basic majority was large enough to save it, though on this occasion it was reduced to an ominously low figure—eighty-one, which was far lower than any other in the life of that Parliament. Thirty-three Conservatives had voted with the opposition, including Harold Macmillan, who would one day himself be prime minister, and Quintin Hogg, who as Lord Hailsham would one day occupy the posts of both lord chancellor and chairman of the Conservative Party Association. This was an undoubted shock to the prime minister's authority, underlined by the chorus of Labour back-benchers howling "Go! Go! Go!" as he hurried from the House.

Afterward, in a private discussion with Churchill, Chamberlain admitted that he felt he could not carry on leading a one-party government, that a national government embracing members of all parties must be formed to prosecute the war—and he doubted if the Labour leaders would agree to serve under his direction.

But the prime minister's spirits had recovered somewhat by

the following morning, and his personal position did not strike him as quite so uncertain. Thus when, flanked by Churchill on one side and the foreign secretary, Lord Halifax, on the other, he proposed the formation of a national government to the Labour leaders, Mr. Attlee and Mr. Greenwood, he omitted any mention of the possibility of his own resignation. The Labour leaders listened politely, saying that they must consult with their own colleagues before giving their decision upon so momentous a course.

But their evident reluctance to serve under Chamberlain was obvious. After Attlee and Greenwood had left, some discussion took place between the three Cabinet ministers, during which Chamberlain hinted that in view of Labour's past consistent hostility to Churchill's aggressive policies and also in view of his reputation for imaginative but often impractical action, the king would prefer Halifax to Churchill as his first minister. On this note the discussion ended, but it was evident that during the next twenty-four hours significant changes in the direction of the war must take place.

Friday, May 10, 1940, did indeed produce significant changes in all aspects of the war, one so overwhelming that the events in Whitehall passed almost unnoticed. The expected spring offensive of the German Wehrmacht began at half past five in the morning, and by eight o'clock both Belgium and Holland had been invaded, Rotterdam was under air attack, and German parachutists were dropping on key points along an obviously carefully planned attack route. As telegrams poured into Whitehall from the admiralty and Royal Air Force headquarters, from Lord Gort commanding the British Expeditionary Force (BEF) in France, from Paris and Brussels, and direct from Queen Wilhelmina of the Netherlands to King George V, the startled prime minister called a hurried Cabinet meeting.

Mr. Chamberlain's first reaction was one of personal elation. With so vast and indeed world-shaking events taking place on the Continent, minor matters such as changes in the British cabinet were unimportant, and all must now sink their differences and work together—still under his direction—to fight the common foe. He was both upset and angry when one of his closest supporters in the past, the lord privy seal, Mr. Kingsley Wood, told him in cold and forthright terms that the opposite was true and that the need for a national government under a new leader was now even more imperative than it had been twelve hours before. And as Mr. Chamberlain pondered this latest defection from his ranks, the reply of the Labour leaders was delivered: they would not serve in any government of which he was the leader.

At eleven o'clock, he sent for Lord Halifax and Mr. Churchill in order to decide which of them he should recommend to the king as his successor when his own resignation had been accepted.

"I have had many important interviews in my public life," Mr. Churchill later wrote, "and this was certainly the most important. Usually I talk a great deal, but on this occasion I was silent."

It must have been a remarkable scene. Mr. Chamberlain, still icily certain of the rightness of his every action since taking office but prepared to yield in the face of such incomprehensible hostility, and now certain that his preference for Lord Halifax was justifiable; Churchill silent, feeling no doubt the weight of history already pressing about him; Halifax uncertain, his sense of duty unsustained by any overwhelming or driving ambition. It was, as Churchill wrote "a very long pause. . . . It certainly seemed longer than the two minutes which one observes in the commemorations of Armistice Day."

It was broken at last by Halifax. It would be, he said, very difficult for him to direct the War Cabinet from outside the House of Commons, where all the major decisions must be debated, and from which, as a member of the House of Lords, he was barred. (It should be remembered that these were the days before a peer of the realm could resign his title.) He spoke in this vein for some time, and when he had finished, it was evident that Mr. Churchill would be recommended to His Majesty. There was a little more desultory conversation after which the three men parted and Mr. Churchill returned to the admiralty.

During the rest of that morning and the afternoon, the first lord stayed in his office, dealing with the growing flood of cables and telegrams; watching with astonishment and some alarm the movement of arrows and blocks on the huge map of France and the Lowlands indicating the advance of Hitler's armies; and awaiting the call to Buckingham Palace.

It came late in the afternoon, and at six o'clock Mr. Churchill was shown into the presence of the king he was to serve so devotedly through such crucial years.

"I suppose you don't know why I have sent for you?" the king asked, smiling.

"Sir, I simply couldn't imagine why," replied Churchill, matching his mood.

"I want to ask you to form a government."

So began the premiership of one of the most remarkable men in British history, a man of fiery temper but of quick, sometimes romantic passions, of driving ambition but of an even more powerful love of his country; a man capable of tenacious intellectual argument but accepting persuasion and correction; a lover of literature, of good food and drink, but also of strenuous action, of power, and of danger.

A man with confidence in his own ability and in his own fortune.

"I cannot conceal from the reader of this truthful account that as I went to bed at about 3 A.M., I was conscious of a profound sense of relief. At last I had the authority to give directions over the whole scene. I felt as if I were walking with destiny, and that all my past life had been but a preparation for this hour and for this trial."

CHAPTER ONE

Few prime ministers in British history have taken office with
so powerful claims to the support not only of Parliament but
of the country as a whole, as did Winston Churchill. His
warnings over the previous years of the dangers posed to
democracy by the dictator powers, especially by Hitler's
Germany, had been so consistent and so numerous—and as
the events of that very day demonstrated, so justified—that
no one could deny his political acumen. Neither, in view of
his repeated attacks upon the leaders of his own party in
government, could he be accused of undue Conservative
bias—a telling point in his immediate task, which was to form
a national government.

As a result, within hours of taking office he had gathered a
War Cabinet consisting of three Conservative ministers and
two Labour ministers, while the three next important ministe-
rial posts—those of the three services—were taken by senior
members of the Conservative, Labour, and Liberal parties.
No one refused office under him, and those who had held
office under Mr. Chamberlain and were now invited to return
to the back benches did so without complaint and, so far as
could be seen, without animosity. As day followed day during
those epochal four weeks in May and early June, personal
ambitions were to be submerged in the national emergency.

This gave Mr. Churchill such power and prestige that upon
his presentation to Parliament of his new administration, he
could paint a picture of the immediate future in the most
somber terms and yet, when the text of his speech reached the
public, inspire an instant and enthusistic response. He had, he
proclaimed, nothing to offer the country "but blood, toil,
tears, and sweat."

You ask, what is our policy? I will say; it is to wage
war by sea, land, and air, with all our might and all the

strength that God can give us; to wage war against a monstrous tyranny never surpassed in the dark, lamentable catalogue of human crime. That is our policy. You ask, what is our aim? I can answer in one word: Victory—victory at all costs, victory in spite of all terror; victory however long and hard the road may be, for without victory there is no survival.

And having received the unanimous support of Parliament, he then proposed an adjournment of the House for a week to allow himself and his new colleagues to settle into their new posts and face the tasks ahead.

These grew in number and size as every hour passed. At first the attention of the new Cabinet was focused on home affairs, on attempting to make good some of the time lost during the months of empty optimism of the Phony War— those twilight months that followed the defeat of Poland, when nothing seemed to happen—but by the end of their first week in office, the disasters in France were mounting and compelled the attention of the entire country, indeed, the entire world.

On May 10 the Wehrmacht and the Luftwaffe had launched an offensive of a power and speed never seen before, an offensive only envisaged by such military theorists as Liddell Hart and Fuller in England, Guderian in Germany, and perhaps de Gaulle in France. Within five days, the Dutch army had capitulated, and German panzer divisions had broken through the French defenses and crossed the Meuse just north of Sedan—having knifed through the supposedly unpassable Ardennes—and thus turned the flank of the main French defenses, the Maginot line. To the north two French armies together with the Belgian Army and the British Expeditionary Force had been outflanked, while immediately in front of the German spearheads, the French Ninth Army was already breaking up, its communications wrecked, its line of retreat threatened.

Refugees choked the roads, harried by Luftwaffe fighters, bullied by frightened and demoralized soldiers or gendarmes of their own side, forced into the ditches by strange, ominous foreign vehicles manned by blond young giants who waved triumphantly at them and rarely did them deliberate harm but

German Parachutist

left in their wake an impression of total invincibility. By the evening of May 15, German panzer divisions were reported only twelve miles from Laon, and when M. Daladier, French minister of national defense, ordered a counterattack, the commander in chief, General Gamelin, replied that he had no available reserves—a declaration of inadequacy that he followed the next morning by announcing that he could no longer take responsibility for the defense of Paris. At the same time he ordered a general retreat of all French forces from Belgium, thereby forcing the British troops who had reached their advance positions along the Dyle to withdraw or face encirclement.

Pz. Kpfw. III

That afternoon Churchill flew to Paris accompanied by the vice-chief of the Imperial General Staff, General Sir John Dill, and the head of the military wing of the War Cabinet, Maj. Gen. H. L. "Pug" Ismay. He had been awakened the previous morning by a telephone call from the French premier, Paul Reynaud, who had announced dolefully, "We have been defeated. We are beaten; we have lost the battle!" But Churchill had considered this bleak prognostication the result of French volatility of spirit, especially when later in the day he had himself rung General Georges, commanding the northern group of armies, who assured him that the gap at Sedan was being plugged—an impression reinforced by a telegram from General Gamelin couched in similar vein.

But by the morning of the 16th, it had become obvious that Paul Reynaud's diagnosis might prove more accurate in the end than the French generals'—if only because French political morale was evidently wilting at an ever-increasing rate; and at a hurriedly convened Cabinet meeting, it was agreed that Mr. Churchill should cross the Channel, both to endeavor to find out exactly what was happening and also perhaps to instill some of his own resolve into his over-strained compeer.

At half past five that afternoon he was shown into a splendid room at the Quai d'Orsay, to be greeted despondently by Reynaud, Daladier, and Gamelin. Some indication of the tension in which the conference took place is given by the fact that at no time was anyone invited to sit down. For the first five minutes General Gamelin outlined the military position as he saw it—the broken front, the outflanking of the main French defenses in the Maginot line, the destruction of the Ninth Army, the danger of encirclement of the armies in the north.

At this point Churchill broke in with the obvious question as to the position of the strategic reserve, held back to strike at just such a penetration. "Ou est la masse de manoeuvre?"

The reply was laconic, negative—and blindingly revealing. With a shrug and a shake of his head, the military commander in chief of the nation that had for two centuries proclaimed itself the foremost military power in the world, replied "Aucune!"

There *was* no strategic reserve. The main strength of the French army had been packed into the Maginot line—which had been built to render their presence in it in large numbers unnecessary—and now they were penned immobile in their own fortifications, while enemy spearheads ravaged the countryside behind them. It was, as Mr. Churchill later wrote, one of the greatest surprises of his life.

But all was surely not lost. There were still considerable French forces to the south of the German breakthrough, and even larger forces—including the British Expeditionary Force —to the north, and between them could they not first maneuver to channel and then contain the German breakthrough, then counterattack from both north and south, and thus cut the advanced enemy spearheads off from their main base and sources of supply and support?

This was undoubtedly the most logical course to follow, but in the depths of their despondency, the French were reluctant to admit its practicability. It was, they claimed, the inadequacy of the Allied air strength and consequent domination of the skies by the Luftwaffe that rendered such a plan uncertain, so unless Mr. Churchill were to abandon his claim that the main fighter strength of the RAF must remain in Britain itself to guard the homeland, there was little choice for the Allies but to resign themselves to the fact that German forces would be either on the Channel coast or in Paris—or both—in a few days. As for the British Expeditionary Force, it probably faced the same dispersal and destruction as had overcome the French Ninth Army, and presumably the other formations would suffer the same fate unless a general armistice saved them from actual physical destruction.

It took Mr. Churchill only a few minutes to make up his mind. Under no circumstances would he cut the strength of the metropolitan air defense force below the twenty-five squadrons that the head of fighter command, Air Chief Marshal Sir Hugh Dowding, had assured him was the minimum necessary to defend London, but this did leave a surplus of ten squadrons. He sent an immediate cable to London and at half past eleven that night was able to inform Paul Reynaud that the squadrons would be available by the morning. Then he retired to the Paris embassy and slept through the sporadic fire of antiaircraft guns beating off a few minor Luftwaffe attacks on the French capital.

By the following morning he was back in Whitehall, reporting his experiences to the Cabinet, and considering the position of the British army in France.

There was no doubt that the plan to channel, counterattack, and cut off the German spearheads was the right one to pursue, but he must bear in mind the distinct possibility that French pugnacity did not match his own and that French generalship, already revealed as inadequate, might lack both the expertise and resolution to carry the plan through to success—in which case the only army that Britain possessed would be lost and the island left defenseless in the face of triumphant German forces.

It was time Mr. Churchill closely examined the state and condition of the British Expeditionary Force and the competence of its leaders.

The commander in chief of the British army in France was a fifty-four-year-old ex-Grenadier Guardsman, General Lord Gort, who had won the Military Cross, the Distinguished Service Order (with two bars), and the Victoria Cross during the First World War and had risen to become the head of the British army—chief of the Imperial General Staff—in 1937, a post he relinquished upon the outbreak of war in order to take command in the field. His physical courage was unquestionable, his military training in the highest traditions of the British army, and his outlook formed and hardened in the elite school of the Household Brigade.

The three corps commanders serving under him were Lieutenant Generals Barker, Brooke, and Adam. From Pug Ismay, who Churchill had known for some years, the prime minister gathered that the first had recently commanded forces in Palestine and thus had had to deal with various aspects of the Arab revolt against the British mandates; the second was an artilleryman reputed to possess a mind that worked with the precision of a well-oiled machine; and the third was also a gunner who had won a high reputation for administrative efficiency, holding during the thirties the posts of deputy director of military operations, commandant of the staff college, and deputy chief of the Imperial General Staff under Lord Gort.

For the moment it was obvious that Mr. Churchill would have time to watch only the performances of those at the top level, while those of the major generals commanding the nine divisions would escape his close scrutiny until the immediate crisis had passed and some of the heat and danger of the situation had evaporated.

But upon one matter Churchill was totally determined: there would be no abdication of power or responsibility from the political to the military sphere, as had taken place during the First World War. In August 1914 he had had a privileged position (as first lord of the admiralty, the same position he had held at the beginning of the Second World War) from which to view the consequences of such an abdication, for the prime minister at that time, Mr. Asquith, with doubtless the highest sense of duty but with a naiveté that was to cost him and the country dearly, had taken the attitude that as a man of peace, once war had broken out it was his duty to hand over control to the military and naval experts and restrict himself to fulfilling their demands. Only the lack of political ambition on the part of the most senior soldiers prevented a repetition of the Cromwellian era, and when eventually Lloyd George had wrested the premiership from Asquith's uncertain hands, he found it impossible to overrule the prestige and proposals of Army commanders, especially those of the commander in chief, Sir Douglas Haig, with whose ideas for the further prosecution of the war Lloyd George strongly disagreed.

No such situation would develop while Mr. Churchill was in power. He would be willing to listen to the advice of soldiers once they had demonstrated their ability to think clearly and act effectively; but he would always retain the ultimate responsibility for selecting military commanders at the top level, for issuing their instructions, and evaluating their performances. It was with this in mind that he had retained for himself the post of minister of defense in addition to those of prime minister and first lord of the treasury.

Now he must watch carefully the performances of these three senior officers who to a great extent held in their hands the fortunes of Britain's only army and who during the next few weeks, or perhaps days, would show whether they possessed the potential to lead Britain's armies to the victory Churchill had promised the nation or whether they had already reached, and perhaps passed, their professional ceilings.

The attempt to cut off the German spearheads failed. Their leading panzers had reached Abbeville at the mouth of the Somme by the late evening of May 20. At this point their line was as attenuated as it ever would be, so four British infantry brigades and the First Army Tank Brigade were launched in a counterattack southward from Arras the following day, in theory supported by two French infantry divisions on one flank and one light mechanized division on the other, while equally strong French forces were assumed to be attacking from the south to meet them.

Only the British forces and the light mechanized division

moved at all, however, and they quickly found themselves blocked by German armor of the Seventh Panzer Division. By the afternoon of the following day, the British brigades were back almost to the positions from which they had started (though the commander of the Seventh Panzers, Generalleutnant Erwin Rommel, later admitted that he had been seriously worried by their attack), and as more German forces began curling around their western flank, they were in danger of encirclement. By the evening of May 23, it was obvious that they must withdraw to the north or face extinction, all efforts by Gort and the other British commanders to get the French to move in conjunction having failed.

Telegrams of reproach and recrimination passed between London and Paris, where Paul Reynaud was under the impression that the British had retreated with no attempt to carry out the agreed plan, just as the French were about to move. One of the main causes for the misunderstanding was the replacement of Gamelin by the veteran general Weygand, who not surprisingly needed two or three days to review the situation. Another was the death in a traffic accident of one of the French generals on the way back from a meeting with both Weygand and Gort at which the details of the attack had been agreed. But both events caused the loss of time—which was to prove fatal.

Despite another visit to Paris by Mr. Churchill and Sir John Dill on May 22, it had become obvious to Lord Gort by May 25 that only a rapid retreat to the coast and evacuation to England could save even a quarter of the BEF. On his own responsibility, he issued the necessary orders. General Adam was to take his III Corps as quickly as possible to the beaches on each side of Dunkirk and organize the beachhead, General Barker's I Corps would move back to hold the western flank with a French division on their right and General Brooke's II Corps on their left—with the Belgian army holding the eastern end of the perimeter. On May 28, as the survivors of eighteen days of hard fighting were slipping back into their positions, King Leopold of the Belgians signed an armistice with the enemy without consulting any of his allies, the Belgian army ceased to exist, and a large gap yawned on the left of General Brooke's positions.

It was as well for the British army that Lt. Gen. Alan Brooke did indeed possess the qualities of mind that he had been reputed to have and also that one of the divisions in

Rommel

his corps was commanded by a certain Maj. Gen. Bernard Law Montgomery. During the night of May 27–28, along roads crowded with refugees and disorganized French soldiery, one of the most difficult of military maneuvers was executed—the disengagement of a division from close action with the enemy, its movement across the face of more enemy troops, and its emplacement in a new position by morning, ready to repulse new enemy attacks.

It was an operation that could at any moment collapse into total chaos; one false move, one mistaken interpretation of an order or misreading of a map, and the whole division would have been lost in the dark maze of the Belgian countryside. It needed the highest quality of training, brilliant administration, and commanders with nerves of steel. Fortunately for the British Expeditionary Force, all qualities were present, and the following evening Alan Brooke was able to write in his diary, "Found he (Montgomery) had, as usual, accomplished the impossible. . . ."

Now the evacuation was under way, watched by anxious eyes all over Britain, none more anxious than those in Whitehall. The highest hopes before the evacuation began were that perhaps 50,000 men might escape capture or worse; but 338,226 reached the shores of Britain during those miraculous nine days, of which on Mr. Churchill's insistence, over 100,000 were French. He had returned to Paris for a third time on May 31, and there agreed that British troops would share in holding the rear guard with French formations and that French troops in the bridgehead would be evacuated in the same proportion as the British. But as it happened, French formations were fighting furiously to the south of the bridgehead (thus holding back powerful German forces that would otherwise have been free to attack towards Dunkirk), and these never reached the sea. And of those that did arrive during the closing days of the evacuation, many refused the chance to escape; the last ships to sail were almost empty. As a large number of the French troops who did get away quickly decided that they did not care for life in Britain and chose soon to return to France—where most of them quickly found themselves in German prison camps—Churchill's well-meant gesture was to a great extent wasted.

But to the British people, the escape of the bulk of the BEF at Dunkirk was a heaven-sent miracle. To such an extent did their spirits rise that Churchill felt it necessary to sound a cautionary note. "We must be very careful not to assign to this deliverance the attributes of a victory," he said in his report to Parliament. "Wars are not won by evacuations." He went on to finish his speech with what was to become one of the most famous passages of rhetoric in British history.

> Even though large tracts of Europe and many old and famous States have fallen or may fall into the grip of the Gestapo and all the odious apparatus of Nazi rule, we shall not flag or fail. We shall go on to the end. We shall fight in France, we shall fight on the seas and oceans, we shall fight with growing confidence and growing strength in the air; we shall defend our island, whatever the cost may be. We shall fight on the beaches, we shall fight on the landing-grounds, we shall fight in the fields and in the streets, we shall fight in the hills; we shall never surrender; and even if, which I do not for a moment believe, this Island or a large part of it were subjugated and starving, then our Empire beyond the seas, armed and guarded by the British Fleet, would carry on the struggle, until, in God's good time, the New World, with all its power and might, steps forth to the rescue and liberation of the Old.

But even after Dunkirk there were still left in France nearly 200,000 British servicemen, mostly line of communication troops and RAF personnel. During the early days of June, it seemed possible that France might continue the struggle, so somewhat to his dismay, Sir Alan Brooke, who of the four senior commanders at Dunkirk had increased his reputation the most (and been awarded the Knight Commander of the Bath as a result) soon found himself sent back to Cherbourg as commander in chief of all British forces remaining on the Continent, with orders to cooperate with the French Tenth Army, which was still in, being between Brest and Rennes.

It was a forlorn mission, foredoomed to failure, but one notable event it produced was the first confrontation between Churchill and the man who was to have more influence on his military decisions than anyone else during the ensuing years. Brooke had become convinced that the French army was disintegrating and that to retain British troops in France any longer would lead to catastrophe. He especially wished to hold one of the fighting divisions back from a position of extreme danger just south of the Cotentin peninsula, and upon this point he found himself talking, on a very bad telephone line, first to Sir John Dill and then to Churchill himself.

He asked me what I was doing with the 52nd Divisions, and, after I had informed him, he told me that that was not what he wanted. I had been sent to France to make the French feel that we were supporting them. I replied that it was impossible to make a corpse feel, and that the French Army was, to all intents and purposes, dead, and certainly incapable of registering what was being done for it. However, he insisted that we should make them feel that we were supporting them, and I insisted that this was quite impossible and would only result in throwing away good troops to no avail. He then asked me whether I had not got a gap in front of me. When I replied that this was correct, he asked whether the division could not be put into the gap. I told him that as the gap was some thirty to forty miles broad at that time, and would probably be some forty to sixty miles tomorrow, the remainder of the 52nd Division would be to little avail in trying to block this widening chasm. . . .

Our talk lasted for close on half an hour, and on many occasions his arguments were so formed as to give me the impression that he considered that I was suffering from "cold feet" because I did not wish to comply with his wishes. This was so infuriating that I was repeatedly on the verge of losing my temper. . . .

At last, when I was in an exhausted condition, he said: "All right, I agree with you."

Three days later the French government, now under Marshal Pétain, asked the Axis powers for an armistice (Italy had declared war on France and Britain on June 10), and Brooke's opinion was vindicated. By a combination of brilliant organization and good luck, the vast majority of the British troops were brought away and had arrived back in Britain by June 20. There was little doubt in anyone's mind that they had been saved in large part by the vision, good sense, and moral courage of Lt. Gen. Sir Alan Brooke.

Despite their argument—perhaps even because of it—Mr. Churchill was most impressed.

CHAPTER TWO

The Battle of France is over. The Battle of Britain is about to begin. Upon this battle depends the survival of Christian civilisation. Upon it depends our own British life, and the long continuity of our institutions and our Empire. The whole fury and might of the enemy must very soon be turned on us. Hitler knows that he will have to break us in the island or lose the war. If we can stand up to him all Europe may be free and the life of the world may move forward into broad, sunlit uplands. But if we fail, then the whole world, including the United States, including all that we have known and cared for, will sink into the abyss of a new Dark Age, made more sinister, and perhaps more protracted, by the lights of perverted science. Let us therefore brace ourselves to our duties, and so bear ourselves that, if the British Empire and Commonwealth last for a thousand years, men will still say—"This was their finest hour."

Thus did Mr. Churchill summon the British people in 1940 to face as grave a danger as had threatened them and their homeland since the Armada in 1588. He had no need to call twice. The danger of the hour served to draw together every class and every degree of man and woman, and the doubts and hesitations that had haunted Britain under the ineffective leadership before May 10 were swept away by Churchill's oratory, by his total dedication to the country and the people he now led, by the pulsing energy that seemed now to flow from the seats of power.

Everyone wanted to do something, and Churchill was wise enough to see that they were given tasks of apparent value even if cooler thought would have revealed their emptiness. A wide ditch was dug across the length of southern

Britain, which kept itching hands busy, though it would hardly delay a panzer division half an hour; concrete pill boxes still dot the countryside today in what were thought to be strategic points but were rarely close enough together to form a realistic pattern of defensive fire, even against infantry attacks; slit trenches and air-raid shelters were dug in back gardens, and although the latter, in large cities, especially London, were soon to be put to good use, a great deal of the energy used to build them in rural areas was wasted. Wasted, that is, except for the therapeutic value given by its expenditure in that time of danger, when physical tiredness calmed fears and served to knit the community together.

Not all the energy was wasted. That expended by the soldiers returned from France or recently called up was now put to very good use indeed, as they built gun positions for what few guns remained in their hands and prepared the beaches of southern and eastern England for defense; and all of them trained as hard as their commanders could contrive, while Churchill himself goaded the commanders, about whom he was learning more and more.

There had been changes, even while the Dunkirk evacuation had been taking place. Churchill had been very impressed by Sir John Dill in his post as vice-chief of the Imperial General Staff, whereas his superior, General "Tiny" Ironside—a huge man with a fearsome reputation as a fire-eater, gained during and immediately after the First World War—seemed remote and ill at ease in his exalted position. With the possibility of invasion to face, it was evident that the position of commander in chief of the Home Forces might soon entail considerable responsibility, so Ironside took the junior post, and on May 26 Dill became the head of the British army.

And when the last of the BEF had returned home in the first half of June, there were tasks enough for all of them, together with some reallocation of responsibilities. It seemed to most people in Whitehall that the most immediately threatened part of England was the south coast, and Southern Command the most vital appointment. In addition to his recent achievements, Sir Alan Brooke had a further qualification for this crucial post. He had held it during the months immediately preceding the outbreak of war, knew the area and its responsibilities well, and had only relinquished it in order to command II Corps in France. On June 26 he returned to his old headquarters to face far greater dangers than during his previous occupation, with less trained troops at his disposal and far less equipment.

His command when he took it up consisted of little but his own headquarters and the three divisions of V Corps, commanded at that moment by Lt. Gen. Claude Auchinleck, just back from Norway. All three divisions had been mauled to a greater or lesser extent around Dunkirk and were short of men (although their ranks were being made up with totally untrained conscripts) and even shorter of every type of equipment, having left everything they could not carry in their hands behind in France.

One of the few consolations that met General Brooke's eyes when he first surveyed the situation was that immediately on his left flank in the XII Corps area of Eastern Command, was Montgomery's Third Division, still in the opinion of its ebullient commander the only well-trained formation in the British army. It was for the time being digging defensive positions on the Sussex coast at a terrific pace, urged on by their impatient commander who was intent upon retraining it for a more flexible, mobile defense of the type that he was certain was the only response to an invasion by panzer divisions.

On all points Alan Brooke tended to agree with his rumbustious subordinate; indeed, his opinion of Montgomery was so high that when he had been ordered to come out of the Dunkirk bridgehead himself, he had handed II Corps over to Montgomery, despite the fact that he was the junior of the major generals there. The immediate sequel was of some interest, too. At the same time that Brooke had been ordered out, Lord Gort had been instructed to leave but before doing so, to appoint an officer to oversee the final evacuation. This he did, choosing the most senior officer left, Lt. Gen. Barker of I Corps, to be confronted almost immediately by an importunate Montgomery, informing him coldly but with considerable force that Barker was in no physical or mental state to undertake such responsibilities and that he (Gort) must instead nominate the commander of the First Division, Maj. Gen. the Honorable Harold Alexander, for so onerous a duty.

Gort followed this advice, perhaps by reason of its eminent worth or possibly even as a result of being stunned into acquiescence by Montgomery's presumption, and the evacuation was carried out with unqualified success. But from his new post as inspector of training, Lord Gort was never heard to express much gratitude to Montgomery for his advice, or even much admiration for any of Montgomery's qualities other than his energy.

It was, of course, Montgomery's energy that first drew Churchill's attention to him, combined with Brooke's sincere admiration—though perhaps it was Pug Ismay's warning of Montgomery's eccentricities that most raised Churchill's interest. Despite the pressing demands on every minute of his time, Churchill visited the Third Division on the Sussex coast and was both interested and amused by its commander's antics and demands. Transport in large quantities was an essential for the mobile force that Montgomery envisaged, and the three-tonners that constituted the army's normal method of conveyance were in very short supply. Very well. Double-decker civilian buses would do just as well, and Churchill should make them available to him as quickly as possible.

Montgomery's devotion to physical fitness was a point to which Churchill would pay only lip service—he questioned whether it was necessary or even beneficial for those above a certain rank. Here he had the wholehearted agreement of an egg-shaped staff colonel who had told Montgomery that were he to run the seven-mile jaunt ordered for every member of the Third Division by its commander, he would undoubtedly die of heart failure.

"Good!" replied Montgomery crisply. "If you're going to die, die now—and we can get a fit replacement by the time the battle starts!"

So the colonel ran—and got much fitter than he had been for many years.

Not that this much impressed Churchill, who at lunch with Montgomery during the visit commented that the general was not drinking his wine.

"Never touch the stuff!" declared Monty. "Don't drink, don't smoke, and I'm a hundred percent fit!"

"Oh!" grunted Churchill pugnaciously. "Well, I drink as much brandy as I can get, and I smoke cigars. And" he added, glaring, "I'm two hundred percent fit!"

But one possible result of Churchill's visit to Montgomery was a quick review of General Ironside's defense scheme for the threatened coast. It consisted of a series of fixed lines, which, by their very nature, must be very thinly manned and equipped. Churchill's immediate suggestion that bodies of specially chosen trained men should be held back in such a series of positions so that 10,000 of them could be rushed to any threatened danger point within four hours met with a bleak and rather tired reply to the effect that neither the men, the weapons, nor the transport were available—a response that immediately set Churchill searching for a commander in chief more likely to do something about the situation than Ironside seemed capable of. So on July 19 Lt. Gen. Sir Alan Brooke took over as commander in chief, Home Forces, and Ironside was promoted field marshal in view of past services.

Brooke's place at Southern Command was filled by Auchinleck, and Montgomery found himself promoted to lieutenant general, commanding V Corps under Auchinleck. Montgomery quickly began a campaign of insubordination against his superior that bordered on mutiny and under other circumstances would have resulted in a military scandal of appalling dimensions. It ended the following November when Auchinleck was appointed commander in chief of the Indian army and left the country. There is little doubt that during this period only Brooke's patronage, Auchinleck's patience, and Churchill's instinctive support for rogue behavior saved Montgomery from the consequences of his outrageous behavior.

Churchill's main preoccupation at this time was the provision of weapons and equipment with which Britain's hastily reorganizing forces could fight off the enemy. Her factories were turning out airplanes, tanks, guns, and ammunition as fast as they could, but the needs were of the hour, not of the month, and could only be filled from existing arsenals—and the only ones available were in America.

It was now that his long friendship with President Roosevelt, and the unbroken stream of correspondence that had flowed between them since before the outbreak of war, was to prove crucial. The two men had become acquainted during the First World War when Churchill had been first lord of the admiralty and Roosevelt assistant secretary of the navy, and their shared experiences and love of the sea formed a basis upon which a firm friendship had grown. Since the outbreak of the Second World War, their correspondence had been regular, and as the situation of the Allies had become increasingly serious, so had their letters. Now the tone became urgent, and President Roosevelt responded immediately.

Under international law the government of the nonbelligerent United States could not sell arms directly to the government of belligerent Britain, but a way was quickly found around that obstacle. An immediate check was made of all stocks of weapons and ammunition not earmarked for immediate use by the United States Armed Forces, and it was sold lock, stock, and barrel to the U.S. Steel Export Company for $37,619,556.60, which, in turn, sold it to the British government for exactly the same sum, down to the sixty cents.

As a result, the hastily organized Home Guard of Britain was quickly armed with half a million .300 rifles (most of them had been packed into their cases in 1918, and the grease was so rock-hard that the rifles had to be boiled to clear them for use), which allowed over three hundred thousand of the standard British .303 rifles to be released to the army, while some nine hundred 75-mm. cannon, each with a thousand rounds of ammunition close by, were sited in hastily dug gun pits in the danger areas.

But the most pressing need for a nation that would depend for its life on support from abroad would always be for shipping —and in the summer of 1940, the need was for naval shipping to protect the mercantile shipping of the convoys. Churchill's first message to Roosevelt after taking office as prime minister included a request that

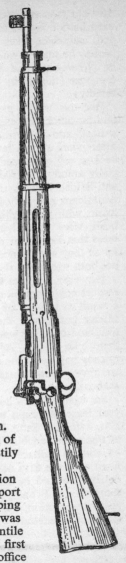

1917 Enfield

fifty old "four-stacker" American destroyers, which had been used on convoy protection duties during the First World War and had since been collecting rust and barnacles at their cables, he made available to replace Britain's destroyer losses in Norwegian and French waters—either on loan or by purchase (though by now Britain's dollar reserves were falling rapidly).

But this was a problem for which even Roosevelt could find no quick and easy solution. Congress must agree to such a deal, and the American people must know all about it. There were quite a few pressure groups to object loudly, some because of organized German propaganda and some, especially among the Irish-Americans, because of straightforward anti-British feeling. Also, quite a large number of ordinary Americans naturally felt that they wanted as little as possible to do with yet another European war. They or their forebears were only living in the New World because of the mess that European politicians had made of the Old, and so far as they were concerned, it was a pity that the Atlantic was not both wider and deeper.

However, the fact that the American public's wishes in this respect could not be met became startlingly obvious when, as a result of the fall of France, the German navy occupied the Biscay ports, and there were only about three and a half thousand miles of water between Hitler's latest conquests and their own coasts. As American naval planning during the thirties had been mostly orientated toward the Pacific, there were very few worthwhile naval bases along that eastern seaboard.

So, eventually, a deal was struck. In return for ninety-nine-year leases of main base sites from the British in the Bahamas, Jamaica, Saint Lucia, Trinidad, and Antigua, and bases in Bermuda and Newfoundland "freely given" as they would be equally valuable to the Canadian navy, America would hand over the fifty destroyers. And if in view of the fact that America would in not too many months be fighting in the same war as Britain, the whole thing became something of a paper transaction, the deal nevertheless brought relief when it was most needed.

Moreover, the Royal Navy crews sent across to fetch the destroyers soon found that the United States had vastly overdone her side of the bargain. Instead of ships bare of everything but the machinery and weapons of their purpose, they found cabins and crew's quarters stocked by a sympathetic U.S. Navy with luxuries almost forgotten in Britain after ten months of war. Cigarettes, matches, blankets, sheets, and pillows filled the living quarters, bacon, steaks, and loaves of bread were in the galleys, and soap, toothpaste, and towels awaited them in the washrooms.

The ships themselves performed their duty during the bitter months of the Battle of the Atlantic, though they were not the best of ships in rough weather. In the winter gales of the North Atlantic, they were hideously uncomfortable, with a roll that put one startled observer in mind of a windshield wiper at high speed and a turning circle as wide as that of a battleship, during which they inevitably caught at least one of the huge Atlantic rollers broadside. This led to the smashing of the glass panels to the low bridges, and the whole maneuver had to be completed by quartermasters and officers waist-deep in boiling seas, clinging for dear life to stanchions, wheels, or the jagged glass edges of the screens. The hands of the survivors still bear the scars of some of their more traumatic experiences.

But the ships filled the gap; without them, the Battle of the Alantic—the only conflict, Churchill later admitted, that caused him sleepless nights—might have been lost, and the only bastion of democracy still standing against Hitler starved into surrender.

So as week followed week during that incredible summer of 1940, Britain's position became if not more secure, at least less desperate. Thousands of civilians who drilled in the Home Guard during the evenings after their day's work eventually were able to exchange their civilian suits for battle dress, and the pikes, shotguns, and cudgels with which they had first been armed, for the American rifles. Alongside them, the regrouped corps and divisions of the Army itself watched and trained, its new conscripts gradually accustoming themselves to military routine, its experienced regular element absorbing the newcomers, manning the crucial areas, ever busy during those long hot days and short nights at training and more training, while the generals drove them hard and tried to plan for every possible eventuality.

And everyone watched the skies, for the crucial battle was being fought between the massed Dorniers and Junkers of Goering's Luftwaffe and the swift, pouncing flights of the Spitfires and Hurricanes that held them at bay. For he first

Spitfire

few weeks the battles were fought during the daytime, and the skies above Kent and Sussex were patterned with the white trails of wheeling aircraft, pocked with bursts of flame as fuel tanks or bomb loads exploded, resounding with the chatter of machine guns, with the high whine of engines at full pitch, with the vast crash of tons of metal hitting the earth. Then in September the battle switched to night bombing over London and the big cities. The docklands blazed, Buckingham Palace itself was hit, and the king and queen—and Mr. Churchill—went out every morning after the raids were over and talked to people whose homes had been destroyed, whose relatives had been killed, badly hurt, or were missing, still buried in the debris.

And wherever the three went they were cheered, for they symbolized the unity that now bound the British people together. Their Majesties stood for the quiet strength of family ties and old, established truths, while in Mr. Churchill the British people felt that at last they had a leader who would neither betray nor misdirect them. His bulldog features exactly portrayed the spirit of obduracy that characterized the nation at that time, and his sturdy figure held all the traditional pugnacity of John Bull. But above all, his oratory held them spellbound, and his every speech gave them new purpose and new strength.

By the end of September it seemed that the Luftwaffe were pausing in their onslaught, that Hitler was abandoning his plans for an immediate invasion of the island, and that the Royal Air Force had, at least for the moment, fought off the greatest danger. In his report to Parliament, Mr. Churchill warned of excessive optimism but agreed that much had been achieved since he had told the nation of the battle to come. He paid a special tribute to the young men who had beaten back the greatest threat to Britain since the Armada, and as he did so, he ended his speech with another sentence that would enter the literature of British history.

"Never before, in the whole field of human conflict, has so much been owed, by so many, to so few."

CHAPTER THREE

While the remnants of the BEF together with its new conscripts had been facing up to the danger from one of the Axis powers, another army composed at first entirely of regular soldiers of both the British and Indian armies had been dealing with the rather uninspired and often bewildered military formations of the other Axis partner.

On June 10, 1940, Mussolini had delivered a speech from the balcony of the Palazzo Venezia in Rome, to a markedly unenthusiastic crowd, detailing the enormous provocations their country had been subjected to by both England and France during the previous few years, and at the end of it he declared war on both of them.

Twenty-four hours later, six troops of the Eleventh Hussars drove their Rolls Royce armored cars through gaps in the wire fence marking the border between Egypt and Tripolitania and ambushed a small convoy of trucks crammed with bewildered Italian troops whom nobody had bothered to inform of the contents of Mussolini's speech. By noon on June 12, seventy disconsolate Italian and Libyan prisoners were making their way back toward Egyptian prison-cages, the triumphant Hussars were sorting the sixty rifles, nine Breda automatics, and several boxes of hand grenades that constituted their haul, while back in Cairo the commander in chief in the Middle East was reading their reports and wondering how long so promising a situation could last.

Not, he concluded, very long.

Gen. Sir Archibald Wavell had commanded all British land forces in Egypt, the Sudan, Palestine, Trans-Jordan, and Cyprus ever since his appointment in August 1939, and with the outbreak of war, his responsibilities had been increased to encompass Aden, Iraq, British Somaliland, and the shores of the Persian Gulf. The area over which he exerted military command now measured some 1,800 by 2,000 miles and

Rolls Royce Armored Car

included nine countries in two different continents. If the forces at his disposal had been in any way commensurate with the size of his command, he would have been far more content than he was.

Potentially hostile lands bordered his commands on three sides. To the west and southeast were the Italian colonies of Libya and Ethiopia respectively, while far away to the northeast loomed the enigmatic bulk of Russia, at that time an ally of Germany and undoubtedly covetous of the rich prize that lay at the heart of Wavell's command, the oilfields at the head of the Persian Gulf.

These and the Suez Canal, England's essential link with India and the southern dominions, constituted the main reason for the British presence in the theater, but to guard this huge and vital area, Wavell had at his disposal only one incomplete and not fully trained armored formation (it could certainly not yet be called an armored division), twenty-one infantry battalions, two regiments of horsed cavalry, four regiments of artillery with sixty-four field guns, forty-eight antitank guns, and eight antiaircraft guns, while down in the Sudan were three more infantry battalions and twenty companies of the Sudan Defense Force. In British Somaliland was the Sudan Camel Corps of five hundred men, in Kenya were two brigades of the King's African Rifles (native troops officered by British regulars) and two light batteries, while at Aden there were two battalions of Indian garrison troops.

Against him on the west were fourteen Italian divisions spread between Tripolitania and Cyrenaica (and after the fall of France at least ten of these became instantly avilable to menace the Egyptian frontier), while in the area to the southeast comprising Eritrea, Italian Somaliland, and the recently conquered Ethiopia, there were at least a quarter of a million troops commanded by the duke of Aosta, equipped with some four hundred guns, two hundred light tanks, and about a hundred armored cars.

Thus the 40,000 British and native troops under Sir Wavell's immediate command were neatly sandwiched between nearly 200,000 Italians and Libyans on the western side and 250,000 on the eastern, while any threat from Russia in the north was totally unfathomable except for the fact that if it materialized, it would prove conclusive.

It was not surprising that the minor success of the Eleventh Hussars on the day after the outbreak of war in his area—however cheering it might be to the troops—did little to ease the main burden of their commander in chief's concern.

In 1940 General Wavell was fifty-seven years old, and he had spent his life in the military world. He had seen service in South Africa and the northwest frontier of India, on the western front in 1915 (where he had lost his left eye and won a Military Cross doing so), in Russia where he had greatly improved his command of the language, and in Palestine where he had entered Jerusalem and advanced to Damascus at the side of the legendary T. E. Lawrence, under command of General Allenby, whom he regarded as his mentor and model for the rest of his life.

So much for the bones of his military career. He was also a lover of poetry—he edited books of poems and was to organize and judge a poetry competition among the men of his command—an omnivorous reader and lecturer on the art of war, a dedicated soldier and yet one who took a refreshingly caustic view of his profession.

"The main ethical objection to war for intelligent people is

that it is so deplorably dull and usually so inefficiently run," he wrote to a friend. "I see no reason why the human race, so inefficient in matters of peace, should suddenly become efficient in time of war. . . . War is a wasteful, boring, muddled affair, and people of fine intelligence either resign themselves to it or fret badly, especially if they are near the heart of things and can see matters which ought to be done, or done better, and cannot contrive to set them right."

However, as he was so near the heart of things in his own command, he could do at least some things to "set them right"—or at least, he could if given the troops, weapons, and equipment. To be fair to the British government, right from the outbreak of war they had been anxious to reinforce the Middle East command, but before Dunkirk the most urgent requirements were obviously for the BEF in France, and since then for the defense of England.

Nevertheless, during the winter of 1939–1940, some help had arrived. New Zealand had sent an infantry brigade, a machine-gun battalion, some artillery, and the best part of a cavalry brigade; Australia had sent two infantry brigades and some artillery; two brigades of the Fourth Indian Division with their artillery had arrived, and from Britain had come the First Cavalry Division complete with most of its horses.

In view of the forces that might be ranged against him, this increase in strength, though welcome, did not on paper greatly decrease the odds he would face should Italian aggression match their numerical superiority; but there was also another element in warfare in the desert that was more intractable than in other theaters—that of supply.

The desert provided nothing but an arena. There could be no question of his army living off the land in any desert campaign, for the land supplied nothing—no food, no gasoline, no shelter, no civilian population to be dragooned into helping in any way; above all, no water. Everything that the army needed just to sustain its life, let alone to fight the enemy, would have to be taken with it, thus using up manpower, fuel, transport, and food in enormous quantities before even reaching the battlefield. This was a point that Wavell had experienced difficulties in making his civilian and political masters in Whitehall understand even before Mussolini's announcement had been made, and there were high-ranking officers in the commissary departments who had a tendency to read the stores requisitions and say, "But they can't need all this at once!"

Now, of course, all these problems had to be put before Mr. Churchill, and it was thus somewhat unfortunate that the first clash of interest between them came so early.

Within a few days of Mr. Churchill taking office, the decision was taken that a convoy bringing a second installment of some 15,000 Australians to Wavell's command should instead be diverted around the Cape to deliver the men to Britain; so when news reached Wavell that, in addition, Churchill had ordered that the ships that had delivered the first contingent should be used to bring home to Britain eight of his best-trained battalions from Palestine—and that these should not immediately be replaced, even by untrained territorials—Wavell used his influence at Whitehall, especially through his close friend, the new chief of the Imperial General Staff, Sir John Dill, to circumvent the order.

As it happened, regular battalions were almost as quickly supplied from India, and as the weeks went by, the danger to Britain passed its crisis point; but Mr. Churchill had a retentive memory, and all his life had been influenced by first impressions. However, Wavell's reputation stood so high in military circles that Churchill could not replace him on so minor a point, and was willing anyway to wait and judge the man on closer acquaintance. A flying boat was sent to Egypt to fetch him, and Wavell arrived back in London on August 7 for a series of conferences with the War Cabinet and the Chiefs of Staff.

It was hardly likely that the meetings with Churchill would be unqualified successes, for the two men, both of enormous strength of character, were poles apart in attitude to common problems and in background and training to overcome them. Mr. Churchill at this time was at the height of his influence and power. By his courage, imagination, and unflinching optimism, he was endeavoring to lift his countrymen from their desperate plight on a tide of emotion and oratory—and if practical realities tended to check the flow, they must be ignored until such time as they could be dealt with satisfactorily.

One of the practical realities was that although in a desperate *defensive* situation any member of any military formation armed with a rifle could fire it at an enemy coming through the door, the same did not apply in an *offensive* situation, where attacking armies had to be taken to their chosen battlefield and then fed and supplied. As has been shown, in the desert this was even more complicated than elsewhere, and here the tail of an army would always appear disproportionate to the teeth. This was a point that Mr. Churchill would never understand or accept. There were 40,000 troops in Egypt already, an unknown number of Jews—who would surely wish to fight against the Axis powers —in Palestine, at least 6,000 white South African troops training down in Kenya, and a large number of settlers of military age and British parentage scattered all over the African continent. Why weren't all these men, or at least a very large proportion of them, attacking the Italian forces in Tripolitania or at least in Ethiopia?

For military experts of the caliber of Dill or Wavell, it should in theory have been simplicity itself to demolish such almost puerile arguments, but they were faced with another difference between themselves and their political master— their attitude to personal behavior.

Churchill was a politician and a parliamentarian—it has been said the greatest of the century—and he had climbed to the peak of power by use of his parliamentary gifts. Every weapon in the arsenal of verbal persuasion was his to command, from sweet reason to flattery, from mordant wit through irony to sarcasm, and then on down through plain verbal bullying to personal abuse; and convinced of the rightness of his cause, he had no hesitation in using any or all of them to get his own way.

In Parliament these formidable abilities were accepted as part of the daily cut and thrust of the business of government, but in debate with his service advisers—the vast majority brought up to a code of good manners and at least some thought for the feelings of others—the results were not so happy. Already Sir John Dill was feeling the strain of close contact with his unexpectedly irascible master, and some of his sessions with Churchill had left him sick and exhausted.

But at least Dill tried to answer Churchill's arguments and attacks; Wavell listened to them with total immobility, responded occasionally in monosyllables or, even more frustrating for Churchill, with a formidable silence followed in due course by a lucid and congently argued paper that too often revealed some of Churchill's most treasured schemes as patently absurd fancies.

Not only did this situation create deep tension between the two men, it stirred unfortunate memories in Churchill's mind. During the First World War, General Haig had met Lloyd George's arguments with just such a façade of impassive silence, and in his diaries published after the war he revealed a contempt for his political master only equalled by Lloyd George's distrust of the general. Did Wavell's stony response to his arguments, Churchill wondered, indicate a similar disdain? And the thought cannot have escaped Churchill that perhaps Wavell would also repeat Haig's performance as a military commander, which in Churchill's opinion would be disastrous.

But if the differences of opinion about the possible use of the manpower in the Middle East command appeared irreconcilable, at least there was agreement about the woeful shortage of weapons and equipment; and to Wavell's gratified astonishment, despite the situation in Britain itself at that time, Churchill and the War Cabinet decided to send to the Middle East a convoy bearing one hundred and fifty tanks including fifty of the heavy infantry Matildas, forty-eight anti-tank guns, twenty light antiaircraft guns, forty-eight field guns, and an assortment of heavy automatics, together with a considerable weight of ammunition.

There followed a series of arguments with the admiralty as to the route so valuable a convoy should take, but Churchill insisted that risks must be run and the Mediterranean passage attempted. He could not accept a situation where such quantities of arms were taken from Britain and would not be available in the Middle East for the five to six weeks that they would take going around the Cape; and it was quite evident to all that he expected that the saving of twenty-five days by going through the Mediterranean meant that the tanks would be in action that much earlier, too.

Wavell returned to Egypt on August 16 with no illusions as to the problems he would now face.

I do not think Winston quite knew what to make of me and whether I was fit to command or not. He was determined that something must be done to put the defence of Egypt on a sound basis; and in providing reinforcements of tanks and sending a convoy through the Mediterranean was bold in overriding the views both of those who wished to keep all armoured forces for home defence . . . and of the First Sea Lord.

On certain details the P.M. was difficult. He did his best to make me move both South African and West African troops from East Africa to Egypt or the Sudan; and he never realised the necessity for full equipment before committing troops to battle. I remember his arguing that because a comparatively small number of mounted Boers had held up a British division in 1899 or 1900, it was unnecessary for the South African Brigade to have much more equipment than rifles before taking the field in 1940. In fact I found that Winston's tactical ideas had to some extent crystallised at the South African War, just as his ideas on India's political problems . . . had not advanced much from his impression as a subaltern in the nineties. . . .

I am pretty sure that he considered my replacement by someone who was more likely to share his ideas, but could not find any good reason to do so.

Unfortunately, there then occurred an incident that, although it did not in fact lead to Wavell's dismissal, did even more to strain relations between Britain's prime minister and the commander of Britain's only army in the field.

Quite early in July it had become obvious that even if the Italians in Tripolitania and Libya seemed to be showing little signs of aggression, those under the duke of Aosta in Ethiopia were slightly more enterprising. Caproni bombers had attacked Port Sudan on the Red Sea coast, Atbara the inland road junction, Kassala near the Sudan border with Ethiopia, and Kurmuk further south—but there had been little ground activity. However, on July 4 at both Kassala and Gallabat (nearly 200 miles to the south) the isolated companies of the Sudan Defense Force and the single platoon of the Eastern Arab Corps had been attacked by, respectively, two Italian brigades with tanks and artillery and one complete infantry battalion. Not surprisingly, they retreated after a token but spirited defense.

Nine days later, Italian forces also attacked the British outpost of Moyale with a force estimated at above battalion strength, pushing the platoon of native troops out, and at

Caproni 314

about the same time a squadron of the Royal Navy under Vice Adm. Sir Andrew Cunningham met a squadron under the Italian Ammiraglio Campioni, off the Calabrian coast, which after a brief exchange of shots disappeared into a convenient and timely patch of fog.

And after each of these incidents, Mussolini had proclaimed to the world that Italian forces had won yet another striking and significant victory against the feeble and ineffective power of the decadent British empire. The claims would have been laughable had they not also been irritating.

Now something more serious occurred.

With the fall of France and the acceptance of the armistice by most of the French colonies, British Somaliland had become an enclave on the Gulf of Aden entirely surrounded by hostile lands, and here the duke of Aosta felt he could easily win himself an inexpensive victory. For this purpose he massed along the border twenty-six Italian and colonial battalions, twenty-one batteries of artillery, over fifty light tanks and armored cars, plus five groups of irregulars, and on August 3 sent them forward in a three-pronged offensive to eject the British forces into the sea.

Against this force stood four infantry battalions and one light battery of four 3.7-inch howitzers, all under command of a lieutenant colonel of the Royal Marines, who was hastily promoted to brigadier. He had no aircraft at his disposal and only one possible line of defense—and this so precarious that he accepted with gratitude an offer from H.M.A.S. Hobart, one of the naval contingent in the Red Sea standing by to aid the inevitable evacuation, of a three-pounder saluting gun with thirty rounds of ammunition with which to hold one post. Mounted on an oil drum and served by a petty officer and two stokers, it did yeoman service until the whole position was outflanked by streams of infiltrating Italian troops, covered by tanks and led by armored cars.

By this time a more senior officer had arrived to take charge. Maj. Gen. A. R. Godwin-Austen had been en route to East Africa to command the Second African Division when he had been diverted to British Somaliland, where he found the Battle of Tug Argan already being fought. The positions of the defenders were already partly overrun and outflanked by the comparatively massive forces against them, and it was obvious that retreat was the only alternative to piecemeal destruction.

There ensued a brief exchange of signals with Cairo, a well-organized withdrawal from the defense line during which the outflanked post with its naval gunners was wiped out, and a properly conducted fighting retreat to Berbera in which British casualties were kept to a minimum but the Italians made to pay for every step of the way. In the meantime the evacuation of civilians had taken place, and as the ferries moved out, British and Australian naval units closed in to use their guns in the final perimeter battles and to pick up the last of the troops as they reached the coast. By August 18 some 7,00 souls (including the civilians), had been evacuated, the defense of British Somaliland had cost the British 260 casualties (of which some were later to be recovered), and as the Italian command was at that time broadcasting figures of their own losses, General Godwin-Austen had the satisfaction of knowing that his force had inflicted losses of 2,052 in dead and wounded on the enemy, together with the destruction of quite a lot of enemy equipment.

The whole operation had undoubtedly been carried out with great skill and efficiency, and the cooperation between the Royal Navy and the army had been professional in the extreme.

But it did not seem like that to Mr. Churchill. Already irritated by Mussolini's previous boasts, Churchill's reaction when Il Duce loudly trumpeted his army's victory over the

British, claiming that Italian forces now exercised a "total blockade" of all British possessions in the Mediterranean and Africa, was explosive. With the round accusation that there were generals in Africa who deserved to be shot, he interpreted the low casualty figures on the British side as evidence of sheer cowardice, and sent a red-hot cable to Wavell—who had only just arrived back in Cairo from London—demanding Godwin-Austen's suspension and the immediate assembly of a court of inquiry into an episode that he clearly regarded as disgraceful.

Wavell's reply, pointing out that the troops had fought well and hard and that the general had acted with admirable efficiency and dispatch, ended with the words, "A big butcher's bill is not necessarily evidence of good tactics!" It was an admonition that struck Churchill almost dumb with fury. The great neck flushed, the jaw clenched, the baby blue eyes glowered, and Sir John Dill who had handed Churchill the message later wrote that he had never seen him so angry; and if the anger was to evaporate in the press of events, the memory was to linger, to augment the disfavor in which Wavell was always to stand.

In his dissatisfaction with the performance of some of the generals—Wavell and Godwin-Austen among them—Churchill asked both Pug Ismay and Alan Brooke for their opinions on several of their fellows, often demanding in some annoyance, "But where are our *young* generals?"

It is difficult to judge whether he believed their answers, but he may have done so as it seems to have been the accepted opinion among high-ranking army officers. Their opinion was that the most promising of the generation of soldiers that should now be reaching general rank had been slaughtered in the trenches of the western front during the First World War. But this would seem to be rather an easy and fallacious explanation in view of the fact that German losses on the western front had been just as great in proportion to population (if not actually greater) as those of Britain; yet on the outbreak of the Second World War, Hitler had at his command generals of the caliber of von Bock and von Leeb, Manstein, Reichenau, Rommel and Blankowitz, to name but a few.

There would seem to have been two halves to the real

answer to Churchill's question, one being that the British army had exactly the number of generals as it had posts for, and only battle would demonstrate whether or not they were capable of filling those posts; and the other was that if Britain had wanted better generals than Mr. Churchill felt she had, then she should have been prepared to pay for them. Since Hitler's rise to power, the Wehrmacht had been encouraged to experiment with every new type of arm they could obtain and every new type of formation they could devise. It is doubtless that in so doing, some generals had exhibited weaknesses and been discarded, others had shown unexpected promise, been promoted, and then had led the divisions and corps that had swept across Poland, Holland, Belgium, and France.

But in Britain the army in the 1920s and early 1930s had lived on parsimonious budgets, and so by the later 1930s when danger loomed, that habit of budgeting kept under tight control anything that might be suspected of extravagance. In such an atmosphere, young men with flair and imagination might lose both through frustration, and those with ambition leave the service to fulfill themselves elsewhere.

But not all, and it gave Mr. Churchill a great deal of satisfaction to correct a gross misjudgment on the part of the army establishment itself, and to demonstrate that it did not always know best.

Maj. Gen. Percy Cleghorn Stanley Hobart, D.S.O., M.C., had been appointed director of military training in 1937 against considerable opposition among top military leaders who believed that Hobart's enthusiasm for the armored concept of warfare meant of necessity the denigration of all others including their own. They were mistaken, for Hobart was well aware of the need for integration of all arms, and far more aware than most of them of the need for cooperation between army and air forces. But his was a violent, abrasive personality, and he treated those whose minds did not move as quickly as his own with scant regard, whatever their rank, and cared little for the politenesses of life in the officers' mess.

Patrick Hobart, as his friends called him, had joined the army as a royal engineer, risen to the rank of brevet major during the First World War in which he had served in France, and also in Mesopotamia, where his military career nearly came to an end as the result of a piece of insubordination that typified his attitude to many of his seniors. As staff officer with the Eighth Brigade, when his brigadier wished to make a last-minute change in a plan of attack, Hobart refused to pass the order, and to make sure it would not be sent, he seized the telephone until the attack had successfully followed the original plan.

The episode ended his association with the Eighth Brigade, but in any case his eyes had become firmly fixed upon a transfer to the tank corps—the only arm, as he saw it, that could produce any form of military mobility—and at last achieved it in 1923. Ten years later he became inspector of the Royal Tank Corps and in 1934 was given the opportunity to command the tank brigade in a large-scale exercise—a task to which he looked forward with immense enthusiasm.

The exercise was a total failure, due chiefly to the early and obvious success his tanks achieved as a result of his own and their crews' expertise, despite the tactical limitations deliberately imposed upon them from the beginning in order to uphold the morale of the infantry against whom they were fighting. As soon as this became evident, the umpires—the chief of whom was Maj. Gen. A. P. Wavell—began the most absurd maneuvers in order to hamper the mobile force. Such ruses were employed as officers' wives guiding the "enemy" into position and infantry and orderly-room clerks lying down in the road, as they had been ordered, to stop the tanks passing. At this point Hobart lost his temper and refused to take any further part in what to him had become a pointless farce.

It is easy to sympathize with Hobart, and easier still to see how his rapidly accumulating enemies made him appear childish and ill-tempered in their reports. "Hobart's Tantrums" were the subject of many a barbed comment over cocktails during the months that followed. But Hobart, too, had a scathing tongue and "military buffoonery" was a phrase he often used to castigate many of the army's most cherished traditions.

I dislike all this dressing up. This emotional intoxication produced by bagpipes and bearskins, and the hypnotism of rhythmical movement and mechanical drills. The glorification of the false side of war. This is not the gay flaunting of danger that I greatly admire. It is the deliberate inebriation to avoid seeing things as they are.

This was not an attitude to endear him to the military estabishment, but because of his sheer tenacity they could not get rid of him, especially with war looming and the continuing flood of information regarding ever-growing panzer formations exercising on Prussian training grounds. Hence, first Hobart's appointment to the War Office and then, as a result of the Munich crisis, a much more significant posting; on September 25, 1938, he was ordered to go to Egypt immediately and to form an armored division to hold off the Italians, who were expected to attack across the Libyan-Egyptian border the moment war was declared, if not before.

On September 27, he arrived at Alexandria in company with several senior officers sent to carry out an examination of the entire Middle East situation. He was greeted by the then G.O.C.-in-C., British Troops in Egypt, Lt. Gen. Sir Robert "Copper" Gordon-Finlayson, with the discouraging salutation, "I don't know what you've come here for, and I don't want you anyway."

The tone for Hobart's relationship with Cairo headquarters was thereby set and was hardly to vary.

But in the field the picture was different. Here, as soon as the officers and men became accustomed to an unexpected demand for speed in all their activities, they began to appreciate their new commander. For years they had been used to carrying out training exercises severely limited in scope by the lack of vehicles, signal sets, the right guns, the right ammunition, the necessary supporting services.

These shortages still existed, but Hobart showed great ingenuity in improvising equipment and total ruthlessness in commandeering personnel. Quartermasters and orderly-room clerks who had spent years in comfortable posts in Abbassia barracks suddenly found themselves out working alongside the despised "footsloggers," or even driving commandeered civilian vans with no windshields and with machine guns rigged in the back, along barely visible desert tracks. (One of the results of such measures was that after the first exercise to be held out in the desert, some wag rechristened the Mobile Force the "Immobile Farce.")

But Hobart was not dissatisfied, and as the autumn and winter of 1938 went by without war but with more men and equipment arriving, the formation began to take shape. The infantry component arrived, more tanks, more antitank guns, more field artillery; and many more men spent many more days out in the blue, as they called it, learning more about their weapons and vehicles, about the work of the other arms with whom they would have to cooperate, about how to live in the desert, and about how to deploy, how to move forward and still keep formation, and how best to find and recognize the enemy without revealing their own strength and positions.

Gradually, the separate pieces of the force learned their roles. The Eleventh Hussars in their armored cars formed a wide screen in front and along the flanks to provide reconnaissance and first delay to an attacking enemy, the tank group learned to maneuver for attack or counterthrust, the artillery to swing into action to break up a threatened attack before it developed. At all key positions, the infantry dug themselves weapon pits to hold ground won and to guard the brains and nerve centers that controlled them all. By the middle of 1939 the days of the Immobile Farce were gone, and the formation was well on its way to becoming, as the Seventh Armored, the most famous such division in the British army and one of the most famous in the world.

But there were other changes taking place, and in the middle of 1939, Lt. Gen. H. Maitland Wilson arrived to relieve Sir Robert Gordon-Finlayson. Wilson had been a fellow student at staff college with Hobart some twenty years before and occasionally had had brief contacts with him since, but they could not be called friends. Nevertheless, he made an inspection of Hobart's command and expressed himself satisfied with the command's appearance and efficiency, then watched an exercise and at the end praised all concerned for the manner in which it had been carried out.

Hobart then went on leave (leaving the same day as Wavell arrived to take command in the Middle East), but the developing political situation quickly brought him back, and on the declaration of war with Germany he deployed his expectant force in the Western Desert in case Italy moved immediately in concert with her partner in the Axis. The next few weeks were spent in patrolling and reconnaissance, but as it became obvious that Italy was not to move just yet and the tanks were wearing out their engines and their tracks, it was decided to recall them for rest and refitting.

But before they came back, Wilson decided to hold a signals exercise to test progress. It was a complete disaster, owing at first to a misunderstanding between Wilson, who just wanted to test communications, and Hobart, who thought it was to try out the whole mobile force, followed by the misplacement of an important code key, the trouble compounded by a piece of total stupidity on the part of Wilson's aide-de-camp, who "did not seem to want to understand the instructions given him regarding map references and compass bearings which were essential to enable him to guide his general to General Hobart."

Heat, frustration, and confusion all led inexorably to high blood pressure and to a confrontation over the exercise analysis, which became vituperative in the extreme, grossly unfair to all concerned, and highly embarrassing to those who witnessed it. There followed a short interval during which Hobart wrote a letter to Wilson rebutting the few purely military criticisms that Wilson had made, but these were no longer of much import. The quarrel had become a personal one, and on November 10 Wilson sent a letter to Wavell, which began, "I regret to report that I have no confidence in the ability of Major General P.C.S. Hobart, C.B., D.S.O., O.B.E., M.C., to command the Armoured Division to my satisfaction," and ended, "I request therefore that a new Commander be appointed to the Armoured Division. . . ."

To what extent Wavell agreed with Wilson is not known, but it would seem that before Wavell had left England, he had talked with Gordon-Finlayson who had, most irregularly, shown him one of Hobart's confidential reports; and in any case Wavell doubtless remembered the 1934 exercises in which Hobart's opinion of his own umpiring had been both unfavorable and vociferous. One point was quite clear: despite the vast area of the Middle East Command, there was not room in it for both Lt. Gen. H. Maitland Wilson and Maj. Gen. P.C.S. Hobart. The latter was returned to England and as no one seemed prepared to make much effort to find him employment, was "placed on the retired list."

All this had taken place before Churchill took office, but on August 11 an article appeared in the press by the military theorist Captain Liddell Hart. It was entitled "We Have Wasted Brains," and Hobart's position, as well as that of other armored enthusiasts who had been diverted by entrenched conservatism in high places, was revealed. Churchill would seem to have read it, for he sent for Hobart, talked to him for some time, and as a direct result of the conversation, Sir John Dill rang Hobart and invited him to the War Office to discuss his future employment.

There was a moment of black comedy when Hobart inquired acidly if he should come in civilian clothes, in the uniform of a lance corporal in the Home Guard unit, which he had joined through boredom, or in that of a major general—but that knotty problem satisfactorily solved and one or two others regarding Hobart's new status, he was soon back in command of an armored division (the Eleventh), and he later raised, trained, and designed the new weapons for the Seventy-ninth (Specialized) Armored Division, which drove the Flails, which blew paths through the minefields, the Crocodiles, which scorched out enemy strongpoints with liquid fire, and the Buffaloes, which swam ashore on to the Normandy bridgehead, all thus acting as a "can opener" for the British side of the Twenty-first Army Group under Gen. Sir Bernard Montgomery, who had, incidentally, been married to Hobart's sister until her tragic death in 1937.

It is by no means improbable that Hobart's services would have been lost to Britain had not Churchill taken steps to see that they were not.

The processes of Hobart's reinstatement did not begin until October, but throughout the previous months Churchill's continual goading of the generals—some called it badgering—had hardly ceased for a moment. Once his immediate fury with Wavell's admonition had cooled, he dispatched a long and detailed directive, analyzing the strengths that Wavell should by the end of September have at his command, outlining his own ideas on how they should be disposed, and emphasizing the need for speed in all military undertakings. To use Wavell's words the directive "showed clearly that Winston did not trust me to run my own show. . . ."

Wavell replied in four cables sent over five days, sidestepping some issues and avoiding some entirely. "I carried out such parts of the directive as were practical and useful, and disregarded a good deal of it." But then events overtook the main burden of the correspondence. On September 13, the Italian XXI (Metropolitan) Corps with two divisions and a mobile group in the van and three more divisions in support, all under command of Marasciello d'Armata Rodolfo Graziani, advanced through the wire and across the Egyptian border—against, according to the excited broadcasts from Rome "massive British armoured forces augmented by the excellent and omnipresent Camel Corps"—and after three days of military chaos and confusion advanced fifty miles to Sidi Barrani, at which point it would seem that the whole force ran out of energy.

They had been watched all the way with some curiosity by the Eleventh Hussars, shelled until ammunition ran out by the guns of the Royal Horse Artillery, sniped at every minute of every day by the expert riflemen of the King's Royal Rifle Corps, the Rifle Brigade, and the Coldstream Guards, and shadowed by the tanks of the two brigades of the Seventh Armored Division, awaiting the time when the Italian lines of communication and supply should be sufficiently stretched and attenuated to allow them to strike up to the coast, cut the advanced Italian formations off from their support, and then turn and destroy them.

This, they had calculated, would be at about the time the leading Italian troops were threatening Mersa Matruh, another hundred miles further on across the empty desert. The Italian decision to stop less than halfway was, as the commander of the British forces at the front, Lt. Gen. Richard O'Connor, said, "all rather a disappointment." He withdrew the tank formations, redeployed the support group (infantry and artillery), and instructed the Eleventh Hussars to keep a close watch on every Italian movement between the frontier and Sidi Barrani.

Meanwhile, Mussolini had rushed to the microphone again with triumphant cries, marred only by the closing words of the official announcement that preceded them, claiming that "All is now quiet in Sidi Barrani, the shops are open and the trams running again." This news must have come as a surprise to the inhabitants, most of whom had never seen a tram. Even Churchill was more amused by this piece of fatuity than aggrieved by the circumstances that had brought it about.

However, quite shortly afterward a train of events began that led to an immediate resumption of his goading of the Middle East command—to the stream of directives, demands, orders, and downright threats with which he was to plague the lives of the commanders in the area until, at last, overall success crowned their efforts.

It all began with a meeting on the Brenner Pass between Hitler and Mussolini at which Hitler remained curiously subdued and thus allowed Mussolini to expand upon the glorious victories won by Italian arms in the Mediterranean theater, confident that whatever scepticism his brother dictator might feel, he could hardly cavil greatly in view of the inexplicable failure of the proud Luftwaffe to defeat the Royal Air Force and thus open the way for the final invasion and defeat of the common enemy.

It was only on the subject of Russia that Hitler rose to his more usual heights of vituperation—despite their nonaggression pact—but even then he gave no hint of any immediate intentions toward the east, and it was thus with deep anger that Mussolini heard only three days later that German troops had entered Rumania; officially "to reorganise the Rumanian Army," but no one doubted that the German presence in the country was really in the nature of an occupation.

As a result of his fury, Mussolini first tried to goad Graziani into another advance toward Cairo and the Delta. Then, when the usual polite remonstrances led him to suspect that he was wasting his breath, he turned his attention across the Adriatic, where, for the past eighteen months, Italian troops had been occupying with varying degrees of success the kingdom of Albania.

"Hitler always faces me with a fait accompli," Il Duce announced to his staff. "This time I am going to pay him back in his own coin. He will find out from the papers that I have occupied Greece. In this way the equilibrium will be reestablished!"

Whatever Hitler's reaction to the Italian attack on the Greeks, Mr. Churchill's was both vehement and immediate. "We will give you all the help in our power," he cabled the Greek government, and although General Metaxas was of the opinion that unless Britain could send at least six divisions it would be better if she sent nothing, thus avoiding drawing German attention to the area, the prime minister immediately ordered troops to be sent to Crete, air force units to Greece itself, and a Royal Naval presence in Greek waters.

All this could only come, of course, from forces already in the Middle East or en route and eagerly awaited there; but Wavell dutifully scraped the bottom of the barrel and sent some units across the Mediterranean, while Sir Andrew Cunningham spread his naval net a little further and assuaged at least some of Mr. Churchill's aching need for a victory by mounting a highly successful strike by Swordfish aircraft* from the carrier H.M.S. *Illustrious* on the naval harbor at Taranto, which at that moment held the main units of the Italian fleet.

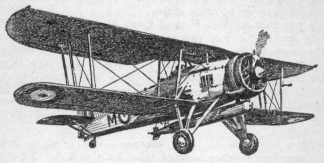

Swordfish

In less than half an hour's concentrated action above the Mar Grande and the Mar Piccolo at Taranto, the huge battleship *Cavour* was put out of action forever and the battleships *Littorio* and *Duilio* for many months. Two cruisers had been badly damaged, and the whole balance of naval strength in the Mediterranean shifted greatly in Britain's favor.

Mr. Churchill was delighted, but inevitably comparisons now arose in his mind between the activity of the navy and the apparent lethargy of the army, and the worth of their

---

*Read *TO WAR IN A STRINGBAG* by Commander Charles Lamb for a full account of this daring raid. Another volume in the Bantam War Book Series.

respective commanders. In this comparison, however, he was unfair, as much through ignorance as through prejudice, for Wavell and his commander in the field, O'Connor, were in fact planning a very aggressive piece of action against Graziani's army. The reason Churchill knew nothing about it was that Wavell was as distrustful of security in London as Churchill was of military ardor in Cairo, a state of affairs that could hardly add to confidence at any level.

One result of this was that on October 4, the secretary of state for war, Mr. Anthony Eden, arrived in Cairo on Churchill's behalf, in order to find out what intentions the command there had with regard to the situations in Libya and Ethiopia. If they were as unformulated as Churchill believed, Mr. Eden was to organize the transfer of even more men and equipment to Greece in order to further a project that both politicians favored, the formation of a Balkan front consisting of Greece, Yugoslavia, and Turkey.

Mr. Eden had long talks with various government officials in Cairo and Alexandria. He also accompanied Wavell to Khartoum, where he had further talks with Field Marshal Smuts and the exiled Ethiopian emperor, Haile Selassie, but all the time he gained no hint of any planned aggressive action in any particular direction. As a result, his cables back to Whitehall confirmed Mr. Churchill's belief, and soon directives were arriving in Cairo ordering the dispatch of yet more men and equipment to Athens and Suda Bay, to such an extent that Wavell was forced to disclose his plans to Mr. Eden in order to save his strength from being so whittled away that no attack against Graziani's forces would be possible.

Anthony Eden had visited Wavell some months before and had established a close friendship with him, so he was delighted to learn of the plans and promised not only to reveal them in the most tactful manner to the prime minister, but also to make quite certain that no leakage of information in Whitehall would compromise them.

Both pledges were honored. Mr. Churchill was somewhat taken aback by the revelation that the commander of Britain's only army in the field had not confided in him, but when he examined the details of the plan, he "purred like six cats" and endorsed Eden's pledge of secrecy to the hilt. But he could not resist the temptation to probe the extent to which plans had been laid for the exploitation of what was deemed a five-day raid into a full-scale defeat of all Italian forces in the area, and although his first cable ended,

> As we told you the other day, we shall stand by you and Wilson in any well-conceived action irrespective of result, because no one can guarantee success in war, only deserve it.

further communications revealed one ominous difference in attitudes between the political and military chiefs. Churchill wanted success in the desert in order to release men for the Balkan theater; Wavell wanted one so that he could turn his attention to the southeast and clean up the situation in Ethiopia and Somaliland by the reduction of the duke of Aosta's fief. Wavell saw his immediate task as that of destroying Italian influence throughout the whole of Africa and thought one sentence from Churchill reading, "One may indeed see possibility of centre of gravity in Middle East shifting suddenly from Egypt to the Balkans, from Cairo to Constantinople . . . ." though perhaps feasible, somewhat previous.

But very soon all criticisms and disagreements were swept away by the astonishing—almost awe-inspiring—victories won by General O'Connor's Western Desert Force. The arc of camps laid out to the south of Sidi Barrani by Graziani's front divisions were stormed during the night of December 7th–8th by brigades of the Fourth Indian Division, while the armor of the Seventh Armored Division acted as a shield beyond them to hold off any Italian support that might come up. None did, however, and within five days the only Italians left on Egyptian soil were the long columns of disconsolate prisoners wending their way back toward the prison cells, while Bardia, the Italian port ten miles inside Libya, was already under threat.

Mr. Churchill need not have feared the lack of plans for exploitation—the whole of Western Desert Force was across the frontier by the turn of the year, the Sixth Australian Division had taken over from the Fourth Indian (which Wavell had withdrawn and sent down to lead an attack into Ethiopia) and were closed up around Bardia while tanks of the Fourth Armored Brigade were already threatening Tobruk. Bardia fell on January 3, Tobruk on January 21. With an opportunism that bordered on impudence, General O'Connor then set his sights on Benghasi, two hundred miles further west across the hills and wadis of the Jebel Akhdar.

His tank tracks were wearing out, his truck engines laboring and their chassis ramshackle, his men cold, filthy, tired, and so thirsty they had forgotten what it was like not to have dry lips, dry mouth, and dry throat; but uncaring, for victory sparked its own energy and the endless stream of prisoners passing back proved its solidity.

Sheer shortage of food, water, and ammunition seemed to demand a halt just south of Mechili on February 3, but then the air force reported massed convoys of Italian vehicles streaming south from Benghasi, obviously intent on escaping around the bend of the Gulf of Sirte toward Tripoli, and by dint of extraordinary exertion and ingenious cannibalization of battered equipment, first the support group and then the tank brigades of the Seventh Armored Division hauled themselves across the boulder-strewn wastes laying across the bottom of the Jebal Akhdar bulge and blocked the escape route of the entire Italian Tenth Army near the village of Beda Fomm.

On February 6, the last battle of this astonishing advance was fought, and another 25,000 Italian soldiers gave themselves up to what they believed were overwhelming enemy forces, but which in fact were less than a twelfth of their own strength.

So it had been all the time. Wavell's force had never exceeded 30,000 men in the field, had advanced 500 miles in ten weeks, totally destroyed an Italian army, and captured 130,000 prisoners including seven generals—for a cost of 555 killed and 1,373 wounded, and the reduction almost to scrap of eighty percent of their equipment.

Nonetheless, they were all eager to press on to Tripoli itself, certain that the tide of victory would carry them there and that the enemy was so demoralized that no worthwhile opposition would be met; and with this in mind, General O'Connor's chief staff officer was sent back to Cairo to urge Wavell to allow them to go and to organize whatever supplies he could.

On the morning of February 12, the staff officer was ushered into Wavell's office. All the maps of the desert that had previously covered the walls had gone; in their place was a huge map of Greece.

"You see, Eric," said Wavell, "I am planning my spring campaign!"

The first spectacular advance in the Desert War was over.

CHAPTER FOUR

The demands made on the army, navy, and air force commanders in chief in the Middle East during the early months of 1941 after the O'Connor offensive were such that, as the authors of the *Official History* say, it must have seemed to them "that this war was not 'one damned thing after another'; it was everything in all directions at once."

The intricate political situation in the area was not, of course, all Mr. Churchill's fault, but he did nothing to ease the confusion and quite a lot to make it worse. He had been astonished at the abrupt withdrawal of the Fourth Indian Division from O'Connor's force so early in his advance and when he learned of their destination, wanted minute by minute reports upon their activities. As the division had linked with the Fifth Indian Division and begun a drive through Eritrea aimed eventually at Keren and then on to Massawa on the Red Sea coast, Mr. Churchill was not given reason to fret at their lack of use—especially as an irregular force under an eccentric officer named Orde Wingate had already escorted Emperor Haile Selassie back into the center of his country, where insurrection against the Italians was fomenting. Moreover, well away to the south, three divisions —one from the Gold Coast, one from East Africa and one from South Africa, all under command of Lt. Gen. Alan Cunningham—were driving deep into Italian Somaliland, aiming first for Mogadishu, then for the heart of the Italian East African Empire, Addis Ababa.

The duke of Aosta's forces were therefore facing attack from north and south while trouble erupted in their center. There was no way in which help could come to them from the motherland, so Wavell's plan to clear his southern flank as well as his western was proceeding satisfactorily. In view of the evident success of the operations, there was as yet no direct complaint from Whitehall.

55

But there were other matters of some urgency to be dealt with on other fronts, and suggestions and instructions from Mr. Churchill were soon arriving in Cairo with the regularity and some of the disturbing effect of tracer bullets. Kismayu should be captured quickly and the advance into Eritrea accelerated; extra forces should be brought up to the Delta from Kenya; the "first duty" of the Royal Air Force in the area must be the defense of Malta, but ten squadrons must be available for dispatch to Turkey the moment political developments allowed; the Japanese would undoubtedly be deterred from aggressive posturing in the Indian Ocean by the swift liquidation of Italian East Africa, but the capture of Rhodes was a matter of first importance. Above all, Churchill wrote, "Let your first thoughts be for Greece."

And it was in relation to that last matter that Mr. Eden, accompanied by Wavell's old friend Sir John Dill, was coming out to Cairo for important discussions. He arrived on February 20.

To Mr. Eden, who had just been promoted from secretary of war to foreign secretary (the third time he had been given this post), the position in the Middle East was vastly different from what it had been during his visit the previous October. Then, Italian divisions had occupied Egyptian soil and threatened Cairo itself, while across the Mediterranean, Greek forces were more than holding their own against Mussolini's attempted invasion of their country. The Greek prime minister, General Ioannis Metaxas, was quite explicit that he did not want a conspicuous British presence in his country.

Now all this had changed. Graziani's forces were four hundred miles back behind their own frontiers, and Metaxas was dead, struck down by a heart attack on January 20. Although his successor, M. Koryzis, had proclaimed that the country's policy would not be changed, he had indicated that perhaps more British reinforcement would be acceptable under the terms of the agreement made between Britain and Greece on April 13, 1939.

And Mr. Eden felt strongly that if Greece asked for Britain's wholehearted support, then Britain should give it. His country, in Mr. Eden's opinion, had of late broken or at least failed to fulfill far too many promises, had reneged on too many obligations: to the League of Nations over sanctions against Italy during the Abyssinian War (over which Mr. Eden had resigned as foreign secretary under Mr. Chamberlain); to Czechoslovakia at the time of Munich; to Poland when the war broke out. Now he was determined that a stand should be made and that however inconvenient Britain's promise of aid to the country often called the cradle of civilization might be, it would be honored.

In this, though for slightly different reasons, he had the support of General Wavell. To the commander in chief of the Middle East as the theater was then constituted, the main threat would always loom in the north. Here lay Germany and Russia (though recent developments seemed to indicate that Russia was not such a menace as had once seemed likely), and the scheme for a Balkan front looked eminently justifiable. The dangers to the west and south, which had once been Wavell's chief concern, were now fast evaporating, and anyway Italian military threats had never been as potent as those from Germany. Many months before, when France had still been an ally, General Weygand had passed through Cairo on his way to take up his post as commander in chief in Syria and the Lebanon, and the two had had long talks on the strategic problems that faced them both. They had agreed then—and Wavell saw no reason to believe that France's defection had changed the basic problem—that Turkey was the main bulwark behind which they might shelter, but that while this remained politically unattainable, Greece and Yugoslavia should be regarded as their front line, with Salonika the key point. Perhaps, as Mr. Churchill sometimes suggested, the war would eventually be won by a strike "up through the under-belly of Europe." So when Mr. Eden arrived in Cairo, Wavell greeted him with the words, "As you were so long, I felt I had to get started, and I have begun the concentration for the move of troops to Greece." He had, in fact, already stripped Cyrenaica of all experienced formations and was replacing them with whatever fresh units he could muster.

It is somewhat ironical in view of what subsequently happened and the blame that has since been poured on Churchill, that one of his cables to Eden during the next few days ended:

Do not consider yourself obligated to a Greek enterprise if in your hearts you feel it will be only another Norwegian fiasco. If no good plan can be made, please say so. But of course you know how valuable success would be.

But this note of caution was sounded too late. Mr. Eden was set upon the expedition to Greece, while General Wavell, despite some strong advice to the contrary from his staff, felt that the defense of Greece against the forces that the intelligence services assured them were being massed to the north, was a practicable operation of war.

So began the Greek debacle, but long before it ended the simple fact of Greek involvement was to have dire consequences for Wavell on both his western and eastern flanks.

Station X, the secret decoding organization at Bletchley Park in Buckinghamshire, was now producing its Ultra intelligence by almost daily reading of Axis wireless traffic, so both Churchill and Wavell had had early warnings of the dispatch to Tripoli of significant German forces, including elements of at least two panzer brigades under command of the same Generalleutnant Rommel against whose Seventh Panzer Division the First Army Tank Brigade had fought around Arras. Mr. Churchill took little immediate notice, since at this time General O'Connor's men were sweeping all before them. Also, his attention was taken up with the scheme for the Balkan front. But Wavell noted the facts and determined to investigate as soon as time allowed.

However, other matters occupied him until early March, but then he decided he must visit the front between Benghasi and El Agheila to insure that it was adequately held against whatever threat this new danger might pose. He was appalled by what he found. He knew of course, that the units now in the frontier area were inexperienced and under strength, but he had been misled as to the natural defensive positions for them to hold and the ability of the new commander at the front, Lt. Gen. Philip Neame.

Wavell had hoped that O'Connor would have been able to assume this post, but during the closing days of the Beda Fomm battle, O'Connor had developed stomach trouble and was for the moment in a hospital in Cairo, so Neame had been sent up at the end of February. Upon inspection, Wavell found that a brigade of Australian troops had been placed in the middle of the plain to the south of Benghasi with no

transport and both flanks exposed. The hills on their eastern
flank were easily accessible to enemy armor and did not, as
Wavell had been given to believe, resemble in any way the
impassable land cliffs of the main desert escarpment running
east of Tobruk. As for the troops down near El Agheila and
thus closest to the enemy, these were unblooded territorial
riflemen from the East End of London, and their nearest
armored support was held fifteen miles back.

Giving instructions for some immediate redeployment, Wavell returned to Cairo to see how soon he might have troops
to spare from other theaters with which to reinforce Neame,
and to carry out a thorough analysis of the situation. It was
undoubtedly serious, but upon deep reflection he came to the
conclusion that it was not quite so immediately critical as had
at first appeared. From reports coming in from the south,
where both the advance through Eritrea and Cunningham's
drive up from Mogadishu were proceeding satisfactorily, he
gathered that he might soon have the Fourth and Fifth Indian
Divisions at his disposal, and perhaps the South African
Division as well. More important, it seemed that he had some
time in hand.

If the new German general planned to attack the positions
in Cyrenaica, he would need supply dumps in the forward
area, and for the force that Intelligence said he now had at
his disposal, those dumps would take at least thirty days to
build. Moreover, the latest news from Ultra was that a new
panzer formation—perhaps even a complete division—was en
route to Africa, and surely General Rommel would wait for
it. As it was not due to arrive until May and would then need
time for acclimatization and absorption into the existing force
at the front, this surely meant that Neame would have until
June to get ready to face the threat; and with two or perhaps
three months to spare and at least two divisions to add to the
defense, Wavell could himself make sure that the job was well
done.

But Wavell did not yet know Rommel.

Generalleutnant Erwin Johannes Eugen Rommel had been
in North Africa since February 12, knew quite well that the
defenses opposite were thinly manned, and had divined that
they were inexpertly commanded. He was also impatient for
glory and at loggerheads with his military superiors in Berlin,

who disliked his methods, mistrusted his ambition, and endeavored on every occasion to obstruct his plans.

As he was such a long way from them, however, he decided that he could ignore their instructions to await reinforcement and to proceed with extreme caution at all times, so the first attack in the desert by the Afrika Korps began on the morning of March 31, and it was instantly and spectacularly successful. Within a week their spearheads had taken Benghasi and were threatening Mechili, and on the evening of April 7 a far-ranging reconnaissance column captured both General Neame and—much more disastrously for the British—General O'Connor, who had been sent by Wavell to try to reduce to order the total chaos that had descended upon the area as a result of the depth and speed of Rommel's advance.

By April 10, Rommel's forces were circling around Tobruk (into which the Australian brigades had retreated and were about to begin their famous defense of the port), and his reconnaissance units were already at the Egyptian border. Between the two positions the desert was littered with random groups of British soldiers, rarely of even company strength, doggedly marching eastward (all their meager transport had either been captured or had broken down) in the hope that they would reach friends before being themselves captured or dying of thirst.

By the end of the month, Rommel held the line of the Egyptian frontier and had an advance unit ten miles in front holding the vital Halfaya Pass down the escarpment, while a hundred miles to his rear a motley force of Australian and Indian infantry with British gunners and tank crews were hanging grimly on to Tobruk.

The entire pattern of war in the Middle East had changed irrevocably.

The pattern of war as seen from Whitehall had changed, too, but not everywhere in such a disastrous manner. What Mr. Churchill called "the glorious conception of Lend-Lease" had been passed by Congress early in March, thus giving reality to the idea put forward the previous December by Mr. Roosevelt in one of his fireside chats to the American public.

"Suppose my neighbor's house catches fire and I have a length of garden hose four or five hundred feet away. If he can take my garden hose and connect it up with his hydrant, I may help him to put out the fire. Now what do I do? I don't say to him before that operation, 'Neighbor, my garden hose cost me fifteen dollars; you have to pay me fifteen dollars for it.' No! What is the transaction which goes on? I don't want fifteen dollars—I want my garden hose back after the fire is over."

It must have crossed many peoples' minds that it would be a little difficult for Britain to return the ammunition that would be supplied under this munificent arrangement and also that the ships, tanks, guns, and trucks might be hardly worth the trouble of reclaiming after even a few months, let alone years, of combat—but in another fireside chat the president suggested that if Britain were to fall, America would be "living at the point of a gun!" And he ended this talk with the proclamation, "We must be the great arsenal of Democracy."

The Lend-Lease bill was approved by the House of Repre-

Hawker Hurricane

sentatives and signed by the president on March 11, and its passage allowed Churchill to view for the moment the rebuff in the desert with calmness, sympathy, and an immediate concern to help. The nagging ceased, and to Wavell's repeated astonishment he received a cable at the end of April informing him that Britain's defenses had once more been stripped bare and some 300 new tanks and over 50 Hurricane fighters were en route, again despite admiralty warnings, through the Mediterranean so that they would be with him by mid-May.

But by that time, other disasters had occurred to Allied arms.

On April 5 the long-awaited German attack down through the Balkans had been launched, and by the evening Belgrade was in flames, and an ammunition ship in Piraeus harbor had been bombed by the Luftwaffe. The subsequent explosion almost totally wrecked the port installations. Two days later, the Yugoslav southern front was broken (and Neame and O'Connor were taken prisoner in Cyrenaica). On April 11th two panzer divisions smashed through the the the first of the Greek defenses, and within five days British and Greek forces were fighting desperately at Thermopylae and bidding fair to repeat the cost of the more famous battle there. On April 24 the Greek government capitulated, and the surviving British and Australian troops began an evacuation from what was, only too obviously, "another Norwegian fiasco."

May was dominated for the Middle East theater by three main events: the first attempt to push Rommel back from the Egyptian border; the German airborne invasion of Crete; and the first stage of an imbroglio on Wavell's northeastern flank in Iraq and Syria, which was to have significant effects upon all future relations between himself and Whitehall.

Operation Brevity was a disaster from the British point of view, for two reasons. It had been launched upon inadequate intelligence by inadequate forces, and these for the first time came up against German defenses containing their remarkable 88-mm. Flak gun used in an antitank role. The result was that after only thirty-six hours the British had lost 160 dead and wounded, five invaluable tanks had been destroyed and thirteen damaged, with much extra wear and tear on already overworn engines and tank tracks. Moreover, by the end of the action the Germans held an arc of defense sweeping southwest from Halfaya Pass, with its main strong points built around several more 88-mm.'s—rushed forward now that their value had been so clearly demonstrated—sunk so deep into the ground that little was visible from the front except the barrels.

German 88

"I had great hopes of the effectiveness of this arrangement," Rommel wrote, with a confidence only too soon to prove justified.

As for the battle on Crete, it was, to use Wellington's phrase, "a damned nice thing—the neatest-run thing you ever saw in your life!" But unfortunately for the British and New Zealanders, its outcome was not so happy as that of Waterloo. After twelve days of Homeric conflict fought among the orange groves, the scented gardens, and across the terraced hills, the battle reached its dusty and depressing conclusion on the tiny south coast beach at Sphakia, to be followed by yet another evacuation, another tale of unavailing gallantry, of abandoned equipment, and of brave and valuable men killed and taken prisoner. But at least the whole Greek entanglement was now over and could no longer drain men and material from the main battlefronts.

The third complexity with which Wavell had to contend that month had two main causes, the first of which was Mr. Churchill's old, unlikely, and decidedly un-English love affair with France.

It would appear to have begun during the First World War and had withstood the shocks of early summer 1940 and even the afflictions brought on by dealings with General de Gaulle, who, in fact, was greatly responsible for what followed. His representative in the Middle East, General Catroux, had become convinced that the rump of the French army of the Levant left in Syria "for police duties"—after implementation of the relevant terms of the recent armistice with Germany—was ready and eager to rise in support of General de Gaulle, to throw off the shameful mantle of Vichy, and join the fight against the Nazis.

To this opinion Wavell did not subscribe, shrewdly suspecting that in fact the hard-core professionals left in Syria regarded M. de Gaulle as a traitor and had no love for the British and even less for those of their countrymen who had joined them and had the arrogance to call themselves "Free" Frenchmen. He stated these views with considerable force in several memos to Whitehall, but in early May General Catroux announced that on the one hand his own propaganda had now persuaded the French forces across the border that the time had come to change sides (it had, in fact, merely irritated them) and on the other, that the Germans were themselves on the point of invading Syria, so General Dentz, the new French commander, would welcome help.

On May 18, he went so far as to announce to Whitehall that General Dentz was about to withdraw all French forces into the Lebanon, thus leaving Syria open to whoever went in first, so could Wavell please be ordered to release 300 trucks and the requisite air support to cover five battalions of Free French troops, who he would personally lead across the border?

Wavell's reply to this was a cable expressing his own objections both to the scheme and to this harassment by the Free French, and he pointedly asked if London really did expect him to prefer French opinion to his own—to which he promptly received a cable telling him to do as Catroux wished!

The heated exchange of cables that followed culminated in one from Churchill ending:

For this decision we of course take full responsibility, and should you find yourself unwilling to give full effect to it arrangements will be made to meet any wish you may express to be relieved of your command.

But as it happened, on the day Wavell received it, General Catroux discovered that his secret sources had misled him, that instead of Dentz withdrawing French forces from the area he had moved them to where they could most effectively block any advance into Syria from the south, and that his (Catroux's) whole plan was indeed impractical as Wavell had suggested.

There is, however, no trace of any cable from Whitehall to Cairo apologizing for the needless trouble to which Wavell had been put, and the sad fact remains that the impression left in London, especially in Churchill's mind, was not that Wavell had been right but that he had been obstructive.

And by this time, the other cause of the imbroglio on this front, German intrigue, was having a significant effect.

On March 31, the pro-British regent of Iraq had been forced to flee from Baghdad, and four days later his place was taken by Raschid Ali el Gailani, whose political stance is well illustrated by the fact that by the end of April, 500 British citizens had taken refuge in the British and American embassies in Baghdad, and 240 British women and children had been given safe conduct by Raschid Ali's troops to the RAF been at Habbanyia—and then the troops proceeded to invest and attack it. The immediate result of this was a barrage of cables to Wavell instructing him to "assemble a sizable force" and dispatch it to the rescue, but where the force should come from was apparently no concern of Whitehall's—and this at a time when Operation Brevity was being fought and Catroux was demanding 300 trucks! Wavell's cables in reply held a note of not unjustified annoyance.

A. P. Wavell to Chiefs of Staff   3rd May 1941

I have consistently warned you that no assistance could be given to Iraq from Palestine ... committment in Iraq should be avoided. There are no guns or A.F.V.s (armoured fighting vehicles) in Palestine ... merely asking for trouble. My forces are stretched to the limit everywhere. ... I do not see how I can possibly accept military responsibility.

He went on to suggest that the Iraq problem should be solved by diplomatic action, perhaps embroiling either Turkey or America—a suggestion that caused a noticeable rise in Churchill's blood pressure. Wavell's reply to the curt response he received began:

A. P. Wavell to Chiefs of Staff 5th May 1941

Your 88 takes little account of realities. You must face facts.

As it happened, this cable arrived in Whitehall at the same time as another from Auchinleck, who from India had been watching the developments with great interest and deep sympathy for Wavell. He offered to send five infantry brigades to Basra to help if London could find the shipping—with the result that on the following day whereas Wavell received cold instructions to assemble a force for immediate dispatch to Baghdad for which London would take responsibility, Auchinleck received one beginning, "Your bold and generous offer greatly appreciated. . . ."

And what the cables gave expression to, Churchill was feeling. He had greeted Wavell's statement that there was no worthwhile force in Palestine with the acid comment, "Fancy having kept the cavalry division in Palestine all this time without having the rudiments of a mobile column organized!" This was a grossly unfair statement as, had the necessary equipment been available, such a column would undoubtedly have been formed and used either in Greece or in the western desert. But on the morning of those last cables, Sir John Dill told one of his confreres that he felt that Churchill had now lost all confidence in the Middle East Command.

Now began the operation that would finally destroy it.

The Tiger convoy, rushed at Churchill's insistence through the Mediterranean after Rommel's spectacular advance, suffered only one important casualty, with the result that by mid-May Wavell's armory had been increased on paper by 135 heavy infantry tanks (Matildas) and 82 cruiser tanks, of which 50 were the new Mark IV Crusaders, while the Desert Air Force had received 43 new Hurricanes.

Crusader

Needless to say, Mr. Churchill indicated that he would expect to see the tanks in action against the Afrika Korps in little more time than it would take to drive them up to the front, ignoring such matters as the fitting of sand filters or modifications to the cooling systems, let alone time for the crews to get to know their new weapons. As soon as he knew they had arrived in the Delta, he was demanding details of their whereabouts, their distribution, and the plans for their immediate use. As a result they were soon being issued to the men of the Seventh Armored Division, who were not particularly impressed.

The cruisers, particularly, seemed to possess all the faults of their predecessors plus quite a few of their own. The division itself bore little resemblance to the one that had defeated the Italian Tenth Army six months before. For one thing, it had been without tanks of any kind for four months and was thus out of training, and several of its leading characters had been promoted and posted to other formations. Moreover, Hobart was of course no longer available to retrain the division, and his successor, Maj. Gen. Michael O'Moore Creagh, a cavalryman, lacked both Hobart's drive and his technical knowledge.

Nevertheless, spurred on by Churchill's impatience, the

Seventh Armored and the Fourth Indian Division (brought back hurriedly from Eritrea for Operation Battleaxe as it was named) advanced to the attack at dawn on June 15. Within less than an hour, they had suffered a major setback. The Matildas, which had played such an overwhelming part in the attacks on the Italian positions at Nibeiwa, Bardia, and Tobruk, found themselves shot to pieces by the dug-in 88s at Halfaya Pass, twelve of them destroyed immediately, while another four were blown up on mines.

Away to the south the cruiser tanks of the Seventh Armored Brigade were at this time swinging up toward the Afrika Korps' base at Sidi Azeiz, where they hoped to catch the German panzers. But in doing so they had to cross the three crests of the Hafid Ridge, and on the second one as they dashed forward with all the élan and enthusiasm of the hunting field, they were neatly ambushed. Within six minutes eleven tanks had been completely destroyed and another six so badly damaged that they had to be left on the field— where, in due course, they were recovered and repaired by the efficient German recovery teams. So it went all day, and by evening of the first day of Battleaxe, British armor had been reduced to half its strength, and had not yet achieved its main aim of bringing the German armor to battle.

The basic reason for this failure lay in the different philosophies of armored warfare followed by the British and the German armies at this time.

Since the nineteenth century there had been in the British army a distinct tendency for the cavalry to adopt an air of superiority to the infantry, a tendency reinforced by continual royal interest in stables. Now that even the most enthusiastic equestrian could see that the day of the horse on the battlefield was over, the cavalry regiments had been mechanized. But their prejudices remained—and indeed infected to some extent the regiments of the Royal Tank Corps with whom they operated.

Hobart had put a stop to this divisive attitude wherever he could, but O'Moore Creagh as an ex-Hussar was probably so indoctrinated by the elitist philosophy that he was unaware of it, so it flourished. For him and his men, the job of the infantry was to get on with their own pedestrian battles— aided, to be sure, by those tank regiments who had been so unfortunate as to be dubbed "infantry support regiments" and issued with the heavy, slow-moving and cumbersome tanks

Matilda

such as the Matildas. For the cruiser tanks, however—the cavalry of older (and better) times—the fast charge was the maneuver, the enemy panzers the prey; thus they felt, could they retain the traditions of the *arme blanche*.

But German armored philosophy was quite different, and Rommel had not the slightest intention of allowing his panzers to become embroiled with British tanks if he could avoid it.

In German panzer divisions, the infantry and the artillery, especially the antitank guns, had just as crucial a role to play as the panzers themselves, and each arm was well aware of its dependence upon the others. To Rommel, the task for armor was to find weak positions in the enemy defense, break through them, and then attack the infantry and the soft-skinned rear echelons of the enemy supply organization. Enemy tanks were to be fought off by artillery, and, if the enemy artillery used the same tactics, it was the purpose of the infantry to wipe out the guns—a case, almost, of the children's game, scissors cut paper, paper wraps stone, stone sharpens scissors.

These tactics proved decisive during Battleaxe and, indeed, several later actions. Time and again, the panzers would appear on the skyline, and the British armored brigades would sweep forward first to attack. Then, as the panzers turned away, the British would pursue—and quickly find themselves under the accurate and annihilative fire of the German antitank screens. By the evening of June 17, sixty-four of the hundred-odd Matildas that had been stripped from Britain's defenses and rushed at such risk across the Mediterranean, and twenty-seven of the cruisers, had been lost, together with thirty-six aircraft. There were nearly a thousand casualties—killed, wounded, or missing; and the lines on the map showed that it had been for no gain at all.

The Afrika Korps had thus proved more than a match for the British divisions, and though perhaps Churchill's impatience had sent the men and machines into battle before they were ready, it is by no means certain that the results would have been much different had they been given all the time they could have asked for.

On the last day of Battleaxe, Churchill, distraught at the evidence of failure coming in by every cable, went down to his home at Chartwell to roam disconsolately through the now-empty rooms and the once-immaculate gardens, all now showing the signs of wartime scarcity and neglect. It was not an atmosphere to promote otpimism or even impartiality, and when Wavell's report arrived beginning, "I regret to report failure of Battleaxe," the decision to replace him was inevitable.

But by whom? And how could the removal from so vital a post of such a distinguished officer be achieved without uproar, argument, and the avoidance of any hint of censure on Wavell's performance in his post, which would inevitably bring charges that he was being made a scapegoat for the government's own mistakes?

The answer to the first question was already decided in Churchill's mind, and as it happened, that answer provided one for the second question. He had been impressed by General Auchinleck's personality, patience and competence during the time after Dunkirk when Auchinleck had held the Southern Command, and even more impressed by his recent forthcoming offer to help in the Baghdad affair, so he was the choice to succeed Wavell; and as Wavell had had considerable experience of soldiering in India, the solution would be for the generals to exchange commands.

Wavell would enjoy sitting under a pagoda tree, and

moreover had better go to Delhi straight from Cairo, thus avoiding the possible embarrassment (for Churchill) of his presence in London, where he might give answers to questions put by Churchill's parliamentary opponents that would be best not heard and certainly not publicized. The sooner the exchange took place the better, so the cables and more detailed instructions were drafted at once and sent off.

Wavell was shaving when his chief staff officer came to see him on the morning of June 22 and read him the order.

"The prime minister's quite right," he said. "This job needs a new eye and a new hand."

The changeover took place officially on July 1 but had been greatly overshadowed on the world stage by events taking place a thousand miles away. On June 22, 131 German and Rumanian divisions in three gigantic army groups and including four *panzergruppen* crossed the Russian borders between the Baltic Sea and the Black Sea and were already driving deep into Russian territory.

Operation Barbarossa had been launched, and another dimension had been added to the war.

CHAPTER FIVE

Mr. Churchill's reaction to the invasion of Russia was, despite his fierce anti-Communist views and activities over the previous twenty years, identical to that of the Greek involvement. Britain would give all possible aid to Russia, he had told friends at Chequers the evening before Operation Barbarossa was launched, and when chided upon what looked superficially like an abrupt reversal of attitude, he responded crisply, "If Hitler invaded Hell I would make at least a favourable reference to the Devil in the House of Commons."

When informed the following morning that the invasion had, as forecast weeks before by the British Intelligence Services, actually taken place, his immediate reaction was to instruct his secretary to arrange for him to broadcast to the nation that night, during which he restated the aims of the government.

We have but one aim and one single, irrevocable purpose. We are resolved to destroy Hitler and every vestige of the Nazi regime. From this nothing will turn us— nothing. We will never parley, we will never negotiate with Hitler or any of his gang. We shall fight him by land, we shall fight him by sea, we shall fight him in the air, until, with God's help, we have rid the earth of his shadow and liberated its people from his yoke. Any man or state who fights on against Nazidom will have our aid. Any man or state who marches with Hitler is our foe. . . . That is our policy and that is our declaration. It follows therefore that we shall give whatever help we can to Russia and the Russian people. We shall appeal to all our friends and allies in every part of the world to take the same course and pursue it, as we shall faithfully and steadfastly to the end.

In making so firm a declaration of support for Russia, he knew he had the backing of Mr. Roosevelt, with whom he had been in contact about the British intelligence reports during the previous few days. Mr. Roosevelt's response to his inquiries had been delivered at Chequers the previous evening by the American ambassador, Mr. Winant, to the effect that he would immediately support "any announcement that the prime minister might make welcoming Russia as an ally."

Another person to whom Mr. Churchill had communicated the contents of the British Intelligence reports, and from whom he had received no reaction at all was M. Stalin, and it is one of the great tragedies of history that so many millions of innocent men and women had to pay the price of the Russian ruler's willful blindness.

To Sir John Dill and the other members of the Chief of Staff Committee, the announcement of full support for Russia further complicated their problems, for it quickly became evident that there was to be far more than just moral support entailed. Not only would a large number of the guns, tanks, and airplanes coming from American factories now be diverted to Russia, but even the products of British factories would go there, too—not that this would evoke much in the way of gratitude from the Kremlin.

In one of Mr. Churchill's first letters to Stalin after Barbarossa, he announced that 200 Tomahawks and 245 Hurricanes would be sent to Russia as soon as possible. He received a surly reply to the effect that the minimum *monthly* requirements would be 400 aircraft *plus* 500 tanks, and would Britain and America send 30,000 tons of aluminum immediately?

But the main demand from the Kremlin, contained in the very first communication received in London and repeated in every one that followed was for a second front, *immediately,* in northern France, accompanied preferably with another one in the Arctic. And at no time during the interminable arguments that were to take place for the next two years was there any sign of understanding by the Russians of the enormous complexity of any invasion of an enemy-held coastline. As a continental power—one, moreover, totally uninterested in the conservation of human life—the Russian rulers could see no

Curtiss Tomahawk

reason why Britain then and America later could not simply put division after division across the English Channel until such time as the German defenders were overwhelmed by sheer weight of numbers. After all, they were themselves quite prepared to clear mine fields by just driving infantry divisions through them, so why couldn't the western allies cross the Channel and the beaches of northern France on some similar principle? It was a battle Churchill and the Chiefs of Staff were going to have to fight in the future with a number of bodies, not all of them so uncomprehending as the Russian government.

But in July 1941 Britain did have one army in contact with the enemy—with a new commander. Perhaps General Auchinleck would quickly provide evidence to the new allies that Britain did not intend to leave everything to them—and in order to give him every encouragement to do so, Mr. Churchill sent off the first of what was to prove an unending succession of cables, this one beginning, "You take up your great command at a period of crisis...." His closing: "The urgency of these issues will naturally impress itself upon you. We shall be glad to hear from you at your earliest convenience."

He did not hear, in fact, for four days, but these he passed in some confidence, certain that the tall, ruggedly handsome general would prove just as forthcoming and cooperative as he had over the Iraqi affair, and as perceptive as he himself that *now* was the time to attack the forces opposite him, while all German attention was focused in the east and not one tank, one gun, one fighter, one man, or one shell could be spared for the Afrika Korps, whatever the danger threatened.

Mr. Churchill was to be bitterly disappointed; General Auchinleck did not see the picture in that light at all. He still had the Syrian affair to clear up on his eastern flank and, instead of seeing the German preoccupation with Russia as an opportunity for him to attack, he saw it as giving him time to get to know the force now newly under his command, to insure that it was properly trained and equipped and that when it was eventually launched into action, it was on a well-conceived and carefully administered plan.

In order to defeat the Afrika Korps and clear the whole of North Africa of Axis forces, General Auchinleck considered that he must commence operations with at least two and preferably three armored divisions plus a motorized division, that it would take at least three and a half and probably four months to assemble and train such a force, and, moreover, he felt that a fifty percent reserve of tanks would be essential before he could commence aggressive operations. In view of the breakdown rate of tanks en route to the battlefield on previous occasions, perhaps the last point was not as unreasonable as it sounded; but it did introduce some extraordinary figures into the calculations.

If, as Mr. Churchill was promising, the total tank strength in the Delta was to rise to 500 by the end of October, with another 75 in Tobruk, then this would give General Auchinleck a striking force of only 350 tanks, which he could support with one infantry division. This would be half the armored strength he had said he required, so at least another 500 tanks must be sent to the Middle East immediately. And unless they arrived at the same time as the first consignment, he would need even more time for training the crews and auxiliary arms. Thus, the date for the attack must be further postponed.

"Generals only enjoy such comforts in Heaven," wrote Churchill when his blood pressure had returned to normal. "And those that demand them do not always get there." He sent a cable to Auchinleck suggesting his immediate return to London for discussions.

To this suggestion Auchinleck willingly acceded, though he later admitted that the ten days spent in Whitehall and at Chequers were among the most demanding of his life. There were, however, compensations, and of his stay at Chequers, he later wrote:

> Winston was most affable and terribly interesting. He is a very attractive personality and really amazing for his age. He never seems to tire. I do not know how he does it. He went off for a snooze about 6:30 but was down for dinner. Dill, Beaverbrook, Eden, Brendan Bracken, Tedder and Portal were at dinner and Admiral Pound. After dinner we had a Chiefs of Staff meeting, which started at 10:30 P.M., and we were not in bed before nearly 3 A.M.! When I went off Winston was still listening to martial music on the gramophone!

The phenomenon of Churchill's energy was a matter of astonishment to everyone who met him at this stage of the war, and Auchinleck's biographer, John Connell, later wrote that:

> He was a man in a rage to win the war, to defend his country and the society and the way of life he knew and loved, and to shatter the evil challenge of Nazidom. For that rage, for the energy, the courage and the inspiration which accompanied it, the world can only be forever grateful.

But Churchill's dynamism was not to bring him what he wanted on this occasion. Whatever energy and inspiration he might bring to bear on Auchinleck during those ten days, he could do nothing to dent the general's determination not to attack Rommel's forces until he was ready to do so, until he had marshaled the force that he considered necessary to achieve victory. To flattery General Auchinleck responded with modesty, to argument with logistics and to attempts at bullying with quiet stubbornness; when he departed he left behind a disappointed prime minister, prepared to yield on this occasion to the experts' opinion but unconvinced by their arguments, and in at least one matter seriously annoyed.

Mr. Churchill was an old friend and had for a long time been an admirer of Lt. Gen. H. Maitland Wilson despite the part the latter had played in General Hobart's temporary eclipse. It had been on Churchill's suggestion that Wilson had been given command of the troops sent to Greece, but since the debacle there, Wilson had been performing senior administrative duties on the eastern flank of the Middle East theater, and Churchill thought it time he was brought back into a more active command. He should, in Mr. Churchill's opinion, be given command of the new force to be known as the Eighth Army, with which Auchinleck intended to attack Rommel.

But Auchinleck disagreed.

One of the disadvantages under which the new commander in chief in the Middle East labored was that he was an officer of the Indian Army and had served most of his life in that theater. Even his career during the First World War had been limited to actions with the Indian Army contingents in Mesopotamia, and except for the ten months spent with Southern Command he had not served with the British Regular Army, and thus did not know very well the men from whom he would have to choose his immediate subordinates. He could therefore choose them either on recommendation from others whose judgment he trusted, or upon their most recent exploits.

In his opinion the achievements of Lt. Gen. Sir Alan Cunningham in Ethiopia, where in eight weeks he had led an army seemingly halfway across Africa, crowning his efforts by replacing Haile Selassie, Lion of Judah and King of Kings, on the throne from which the Italians had driven him five years before, had earned him the most prized command within reach.

Politely, but firmly, Auchinleck insisted on his choice, and Churchill, faced with the facts of the case, could not but acquiesce; but the Eighth Army was to consist of two corps, and when the prime minister heard that one of them, XIII Corps, was to be commanded by Lt. Gen. A. R. Godwin-Austen, for whose court-martial he had called after the evacuation of British Somaliland, he was both aggrieved and resentful. It would go hard with all concerned if Auchinleck's choice of subordinates proved unwise.

If Mr. Churchill accepted that he could not dictate to his chief military commanders their choice of subordinates, he was quite adamant that his was the prerogative upon which their own appointments and dismissals depended—subject of course to the restrictions that parliamentary life imposed upon him. Now there was another change he was determined to make, for the choice of Sir John Dill as chief of the Imperial General Staff was not proving as happy as he had wished.

Quite early in their relationship, Dill's close friendship with Wavell had led him to argue forcefully on the latter's behalf against Churchill, and as a result Dill was linked in Churchill's mind with Wavell's disfavor. Moreover, the arguments Dill had used on his friend's behalf had rarely convinced Churchill, perhaps because they made no appeal to his romanticism, perhaps because they were offered with cool reason but never with passion, a quality that Dill distrusted but which to Churchill was essential in any cause or debate. Moreover, of late Dill had exhibited signs of growing exhaustion that contrasted vividly with the prime minister's apparently endless energy.

There was a tragic reason for this. In addition to the strains of Dill's responsibilities as head of Britain's army and of the problems of dealing with his master's volatile temperament, his wife had suffered a paralytic stroke during the previous winter. Consequently during the few hours Dill could be spared from Whitehall, he was denied the opportunity to relax and pour out his troubles to a sympathetic ear, or even just to relax and stay silent. Instead, each visit to his home was an agony spent endeavoring to guess what his wife was trying to communicate to him, and when he failed—which was often the case—watch the disappointment in her eyes, the sad resignation in her face as her head dropped despondently back onto the pillow. For an intelligent and sensitive man in any circumstances, this would prove an almost unbearable ordeal; for such a man bearing Sir John Dill's burdens, it was a test almost to destruction.

Lady Dill died that winter, but the pressures of the hour allowed Sir John little but the leave necessary to attend the funeral, and since then he had found that any time not spent at his demanding duties and in attendance upon his even more demanding master had best be spent visiting troops or conferring with his confreres. He seemed not to wish to be left alone with his thoughts. After over a year in his appointment and over six months in this acute predicament, it was hardly surprising that his mental and physical condition was deteriorating. And chief of the Imperial General Staff was not a position for a sick man.

* * *

After Auchinleck's return to Egypt, Mr. Churchill was for a time too occupied with other matters to take the step that he had for some time considered desirable. He had received a message via Mr. Harry Hopkins, Mr. Roosevelt's personal friend and adviser, that the American president thought it time that the leaders of the two great democracies met—an idea that so pleased Mr. Churchill that all other matters were brushed aside for the moment, and on August 4 he departed aboard H.M.S. *Prince of Wales* for Placentia Bay on the Newfoundland coast.

An interesting and revealing exchange took place on the way out.

Mr. Attlee, who acted as deputy prime minister during Churchill's absence, had expressed fears of security leaks that might bring the German battleship *Tirpitz* out of her Norwegian stronghold in an attempt to sink the *Prince of Wales,* but this was not a danger that worried Churchill in any way. His cabled reply began, "I don't see much harm in leakage." It went on rather sorrowfully, "About *Tirpitz:* I fear there will be no such luck. . . ."

President Roosevelt aboard the United States cruiser *Augusta* was waiting in Placentia Bay when the *Prince of Wales* arrived, and after the exchange of formal courtesies, the two old friends were quickly in amicable discussion on immediate and also far-reaching problems. The main outcome of the meeting was in fact the Atlantic Charter—a declaration embodying principles to which it is unfortunate that the world's leaders have not yet seen fit to adhere—and undoubtedly Mr. Churchill was in great part its author.

So it was a cheerful and excited prime minister who returned to Britain in mid-August, to begin again the series of conferences with his political and military advisers, to make his reports to and play his allotted part in Parliament, to placate the ever-demanding Soviet leader, to organize whatever supplies from Britain could be spared for both the Russian and Middle East fronts . . . and to see that every effort was made to keep to agreed military timetables. In this respect, there were many meetings at both Whitehall and Chequers. At a large number of these meetings Sir Alan Brooke was present, and on Sunday November 16, somewhat to his surprise as he had been there only a short while before, he found himself yet again a guest at the prime minister's country abode.

After dinner, at which Mrs. Churchill, Capt. Lord Louis Mountbatten, Lord Cherwell, and Pug Ismay were present, Mr. Churchill took Brooke aside and led him to his study. There he told him that he had decided that it was time for Dill to go—he would be promoted to field marshal, as had been his predecessor, and appointed governor of Bombay—and it was Churchill's wish that Brooke should succeed to the position as head of Britain's army.

"It took me some time to reply," Brooke later wrote in his diary, the daily letter to his wife that he wrote night after night for so many years.

The magnitude of the job and the work entailed took the wind out of my sails. The fact that the extra work and ties would necessarily mean seeing far less of you tore at my heartstrings. And finally the feeling of sadness at having to give up Home Forces after having worked them up to their present pitch.

The P.M. understood my silence and said: "Do you not think you will be able to work with me? We have so far got on well together." I had to assure him that these were not my thoughts, though I am fully aware that my path will not be strewn with rose petals. But I have the greatest respect and affection for him, so that I hope I may be able to stand the storms of abuse which I may well have to bear frequently. . . .

Nobody could be nicer than he was, and finally, when we went to bed at 2 A.M., he came with me into my bedroom to get away from the others, took my hand, and looking into my eyes with an exceptionally kind look, said: "I wish you the very best of luck."

Three days later, the papers published the appointment of Sir Alan Brooke as chief of the Imperial General Staff, and his long and successful partnership with Churchill began.

On the morning of the day before the public announcement of Sir Alan Brooke's appointment, Operation Crusader began.

One hundred thousand men, 600 tanks, 5,000 assorted cars

and trucks moved across the desert, and on the left flank the huge armored cavalcade of XXX Corps, commanded by a newcomer to the desert, Lt. Gen. Willoughby Norrie, swept across the Egyptian border to the south of all Axis positions, its declared purpose the destruction of German armor and the relief of Tobruk. Despite unexpected storms and heavy rain, the spirits of the troops were high and made even higher by a stirring message read to all of them from the prime minister.

For the first time British and Empire troops will meet the Germans with ample equipment in modern weapons of all kinds. The battle itself will affect the whole course of the war. Now is the time to strike the hardest blow yet struck for final victory, home and freedom. The Desert Army may add a page to history which will rank with Blenheim and Waterloo. The eyes of all nations are upon you. . . . May God uphold the right!

So the Eighth Army went into battle for the first time, in great part with high hopes and unbounded confidence. Only at the top levels were there any doubts. One of the leading soldiers of the New Zealand Division later wrote:

This great approach march will always be remembered by those who took part in it, though the details are vague in memory. The whole Eighth Army, Seventh Armoured Division, First South African Division, and the Second New Zealand and Fourth Indian Divisions moved westward in an enormous column, the armour leading. The Army moved south of Sidi Barrani, past the desolate Italian camps of the previous year, along the plateau south of the great escarpment, through the frontier wire into Libya, south of the enemy garrisons in the Sidi Omars, and wheeled north. Then, just as we were rejoicing in the conception of a massive move on Tobruk, disregarding the immobile garrisons and crushing everything in our path, the whole Army broke up and departed different ways.

General Cunningham was perpetuating the orthodox philosophy, and infantry and armor were split apart to fight their own separate actions. The story of the gigantic battles that took place over the next six weeks has been told in detail elsewhere,* but the names of such desert locations as Ed Duda, Belhammed, Bir el Gubi, and especially Sidi Rezegh are burned into the memories of all who fought there on either side, while one date, November 23, *Totensonntag* in the German religious calendar, evokes both wonder at mens' courage and the chill and sorrow of the grave.

And after it, General Cunningham's nerve broke, and only swift intervention by Auchinleck himself prevented an abrupt withdrawal of the entire Eighth Army and an admission of defeat.

But the day was saved. Cunningham was replaced by an officer from Auchinleck's staff, Lt. Gen. Neil Ritchie, who with Auchinleck's massive presence at his elbow during the crucial first days of his command, saw the tide of battle turn and the Afrika Korps and their Italian partners slowly and methodically quit the field. On the next-to-the-last day of the year 1941, the last covering rearguard of the twenty-first Panzar Division struck a shrewd blow at the nearest British armored brigade and then retired in rain, mist, and depressing cold to El Agheila, the bleak location at the corner of the Gulf of Sirte from which Rommel had attacked nine months before. Thus the Winter Battle was over, the second lap of what the irreverent had christened "The Bughasi Handicap" completed.

Only in the opening phases of the battle had Mr. Churchill been closely concerned. During the first few days he had exuded confidence and optimism, and when the cables began to indicate a growing crisis, he grew calm and offered rocklike support in public for the Middle East Command, whatever doubts he may have felt in private. Any self-justifications about the necessity to replace Cunningham he kept to himself, though he did inquire about Ritchie's qualifications for so important a command, and as the estimates for losses in men and equipment came in, he concerned himself with the problems of reinforcement and resupply.

---

*See *The Crucible of War* by Barrie Pitt, Cassell, London, 1980, and, for a first-hand account of armored warfare in the Western Desert, read *Brazen Chariots* by Major Robert Crisp, another volume in The Bantam War Book Series.

The battle crisis passed, and one Sunday evening at Chequers he lifted the lid of a pocket radio to listen to the nine o'clock news. Reception was poor, and at the end of it there was a blurred and distorted announcement that mentioned both Japanese aircraft and American shipping. Slightly puzzled, he switched off the radio and turned again to dinner.

At that moment the door burst open, and his valet rushed in. "It's quite true!" he said. "We heard it ourselves outside. The Japs have attacked the Americans!"

Within five minutes Churchill was talking to President Roosevelt, hearing the first account of the devastation at Pearl Harbor, of the new total commitment of the United States to the war. And through the chaos of emotions that engulfed him, one blazing fact was clear: the defeat of the Axis powers was now a certainty!

> We had won the war. England would live; Britain would live; the Commonwealth of Nations and the Empire would live. How long the war would last or in what fashion it would end no man could tell, nor did I at this moment care. Once again in our long Island history we should emerge, however mauled and mutilated, safe and victorious. We should not be wiped out. . . . Hitler's fate was sealed. Mussolini's fate was sealed. As for the Japanese, they would be ground to powder. All the rest was merely the proper application of overwhelming force. The British Empire, The Soviet Union, and now the United States, bound together with every scrap of their life and strength were, according to my lights, twice or even thrice the force of their antagonists. . . . Being saturated and satiated with emotion and sensation, I went to bed and slept the sleep of the saved and thankful.

As soon as he awoke the following morning, he decided that he must return immediately to the United States to insure the closest possible cooperation between the English-speaking nations, and the agreement to and practical implementation of the common aim. There were many matters to deal with during the next four days as news of spreading disaster came in in the wake of the Japanese invasions of Thailand and Malaya, of the landings on Luzon and, most painfully for Churchill himself, of the sinkings of H.M.S. *Prince of Wales* and H.M.S *Repulse* off the Malayan coast. But in a storm of activity the arrangements were made, the agreements of Parliament, the king and President Roosevelt obtained, and on the evening of December 12, Churchill and his party hurried north to the Clyde, where the battleship H.M.S. *Duke of York* was waiting, with her escort of cruisers and destroyers.

He took with him his old friend Lord Beaverbrook; the first sea lord, Admiral Pound; the chief of air staff, Air Marshal Portal; and the newly promoted field marshal, Sir John Dill, saved by events from the somewhat stultifying post of governor of Bombay and destined to become Mr. Churchill's permanent representative in Washington. With these men he hoped to establish close relationships with their American counterparts and thus form a basis for mutual understanding and action during what would assuredly be the very difficult months immediately ahead. With them traveled a team of secretaries and cipher staff, and also Sir Charles Wilson, the president of the Royal College of Physicians, who had been appointed by the government as Churchill's medical adviser. Sir Alan Brooke remained in London, instructed by Churchill that it was his duty and Mr. Attlee's to "mind the shop" while Mr. Churchill was away.

The voyage took ten days, partly because heavy gales slowed down the destroyers, and the *Duke of York* had to stay near them for protection, especially as they passed through the dangerous waters used by U-boats returning to their bases along the Biscay coasts. Although the time passed uncomfortably, it was by no means wasted.

Conference followed conference, the talking went on all day and often most of the night, memos were written, decisions taken, cables sent. Mr. Churchill composed three policy papers, each dealing with a different theater of war, for presentation to Mr. Roosevelt and the American Chiefs of Staff, and each paragraph, each sentence had to be examined and agreed by the service chiefs aboard; and all the time, as yet more bad news came in with every hour of the Japanese onslaught, there grew the nagging worry as to American policy.

Obviously, it would be unrealistic to believe that with the facts of the hour, the attitude of the American public could be anything other than "America first." But would that mean a total concentration upon the war against Japan to the exclusion of any great effort against Germany? To Mr. Churchill and those aboard the *Duke of York*, it seemed evident that the defeat of Japan would not contribute greatly toward the defeat of Hitler, whereas the crushing of the Axis powers would make the finishing off of Japan just a matter of time; but would Mr. Roosevelt and his advisers see it in the same light? Already, supplies under lend-lease had ceased, pending reallocation in the light of the events. When and under what circumstances would they recommence?

And yet, despite these worries, according to Sir Charles Wilson, Churchill was like a man reborn. During the days before Pearl Harbor, especially during the *Crusader* crisis, he had sometimes been frightened by Churchill's demeanor.

> I used to watch him as he went to his room with swift paces, the head thrust forward, scowling at the ground, the sombre countenance clouded, the features set and resolute, the jowl clamped down as if he had something between his teeth and did not mean to let go. I could see that he was carrying the weight of the world, and wondered how long he could go on like this and what could be done about it. And now—in a night, it seems— a younger man has taken his place. All day he keeps to his cabin, dictating for the President a memorandum on the conduct of the war. But the tired, dull look has gone from his eye; his face lights up as you enter the cabin. A month ago, if you had broken in on his work, he would have bitten off your head. Now at night he is gay and voluble, sometimes even playful.

The great battleship sailed into Chesapeake Bay on December 12, and the last stage of the journey was made by air, their Lockheed dropping down over the lights of Washington, a revitalizing spectacle for men used for two and a half years to the Continental blackout. Mr. Roosevelt was at the airport to meet them, and by midnight the travelers were all in their hotel rooms—except Mr. Churchill, who was a guest at the White House and in deep discussion with the president.

And already, an enormous weight had been lifted from his mind. There would be no American withdrawal from the

European theater. By midnight Mr. Roosevelt had announced that he was considering the early dispatch of at least three United States divisions, including an armored division, to Ulster, and expressed deep interest in the affairs in North Africa. Churchill revealed plans for Operation Gymnast by which it was proposed to land a new British army somewhere along the Mediterranean coast of Morocco or Algeria, thus "closing the back door on Rommel." To add to Churchill's delight, Mr. Roosevelt suggested the possibility of adding American divisions, converting the operation into a "Super-Gymnast."

It was a relieved and relaxed prime minister who eventually settled down for his first night as a guest in the White House.

So much happened between Mr. Churchill's arrival in Washington on December 22 and the end of the year, that it is difficult to keep track of events. Talks went on all the time—between the service chiefs of the two countries; between Lord Beaverbrook and the great industrial figures of the country (for it was in his role as minister for supply that Churchill had brought him); between the civil servants and the administrators; and all the time between Mr. Roosevelt and Mr. Churchill, generally with Mr. Harry Hopkins present.

Of course, the Christmas festivities were enjoyed as well. Enormous crowds gathered outside the White House on Christmas Eve, and both the president and the prime minister addressed them, and on Christmas Day both men attended morning church, while in the evening a Roosevelt family dinner (which nevertheless seated forty or fifty people) was held, to which the principal British figures were invited. Mr. Churchill retired early, for he had been asked to address the Congress of the United States the following day and had had little time to prepare what was obviously to be a vitally important speech.

There were, he knew, a number of senators who did not look upon the British nation and empire with favor, but what their number and influence were he could not gauge; they might give him a rough time, and he would not be able to answer them with the robust tactics with which he handled opposition in the House of Commons. He worked on his speech alone in his bedroom until after two, and was not totally satisfied when eventually he decided that sleep was more important than further polishing.

He need not have worried. He won a gust of laughter and applause right at the beginning when, after expressing his deep appreciation of the honor they were paying him by their invitation to their assembly, he asked them to forgive him for the fact that "I cannot help reflecting that if my father had been American and my mother British, instead of the other way around, I might have got here on my own!" Later, when talking of the Japanese aggressions in both China and now the whole of the Pacific, he waved his papers aside and demanded belligerently, "What sort of people do they think we are?" He was greeted with a storm of applause, the whole Congress rising and cheering for several minutes.

It was a personal triumph for Churchill, a great contribution to Anglo-American accord; and four days later, he was to score a second such success in Ottawa, addressing the Canadian Parliament. And all the time, not only were the working discussions taking place, but he and Roosevelt were drawing up what was to become the United Nations Declaration, to be signed by the representatives of twenty-six nations on January 1. It is hardly surprising that Sir Charles Wilson had been given cause for anxiety and that he watched every move of his patient with some concern.

The trouble began on the morning of December 27, when he had called at the White House during the morning and been ushered into Churchill's bedroom.

"I am glad you have come," the prime minister said, and went on to tell him what had happened.

Apparently, during the night he found the room too hot so had tried to open a window. The window was stiff, and he had had to use considerable effort. While doing so, he became very short of breath and developed a dull pain over his heart that traveled down his left arm.

There was not much to be found when I examined his heart. Indeed, the time I spent listening to his chest was given to some quick thinking. I knew that when I took the stethoscope out of my ears he would ask me pointed questions, and I had no doubt that whether the electrocardiograph showed evidence of a coronary thrombosis or not, his symptoms were those of coronary insufficiency. The textbook treatment for this is at least six weeks in bed. That would mean publishing to the world —and the American newspapers would see to this—that the P.M. was an invalid with a crippled heart and a doubtful future. . . .

"Well," he asked, looking full at me, "is my heart all right?"

"There is nothing serious," I answered. "You have been overdoing things."

But when they had all returned from Ottawa and the United Nations Declaration had been signed, Sir Charles was very relieved to learn that Mr. Churchill had accepted an invitation to spend a few days resting at a small villa near Palm Beach in Florida, the property of Mr. Stettinius. They flew there on January 4 accompanied by General George Marshall—the head of the United States Army and Mr. Roosevelt's chief military adviser—and although the talks continued, they did so at a less frenetic pace, and some of them even happened with the chief participators lolling in the warm sea.

The party returned to Washington on January 19, 1942, and during the next few days, the seal was placed upon Anglo-American accord. None of the fears that the British delegation had harbored before the meetings now seemed valid. Indeed the Joint Chiefs had agreed under the heading of Grand Strategy that "only the minimum of forces necessary for the safeguarding of vital interests in other theatres should be diverted from operations against Germany." Moreover, the president had indicated in much stronger terms than before that he supported the idea of Super-Gymnast and that plans should be drawn up for the invasion of North Africa by 90,000 United States and 90,000 British troops, together with considerable air support.

As for the overall control of the war, a Joint Chiefs of Staff Committee was to be set up in Washington with a similar organization in London, both bodies to be kept in the closest touch that modern communications could insure. It was a relaxed and contented Mr. Churchill who eventually boarded a flying boat in Bermuda and commenced the three-and-a-half-thousand-mile flight back to Britain. They touched down in Plymouth Harbor.

Four days would elapse before the next series of disasters to British arms would commence.

CHAPTER SIX

If the entry of America into the war at the end of 1941 insured Allied victory in the long run, in the short term it ushered in an era of catastrophe.

The most spectacular disasters followed in the wake of the Japanese onslaught—that astonishing explosion of military energy that in one day crippled the United States Pacific Fleet and in one week put Japanese troops ashore in Thailand, Malaya, Guam, Midway, and Luzon, and sank the *Prince of Wales* and the *Repulse*. Within a month, Japanese troops had captured Wake Island and Hong Kong (on Christmas Day), had landed in Borneo, were ashore and driving implacably through the Philippines, had driven the British out of Penang and Ipoh, and were threatening Singapore.

Perhaps because Europoean and American interests were so much more closely involved, the Japanese achievements seemed even more impressive than had the German invasion of Russia six months before, and they were thus to have for the Western Allies more immediately far-reaching implications. Australia, for instance, suddenly found herself threatened to an extent she had never considered likely—and with her best troops hundreds of miles away defending areas and interests for which the average Australian (and certainly the members of her government) had little concern. They were very quickly to be calling for the return of the Australian divisions from Auchinleck's command to somewhere nearer home.

But for the moment the call was resisted, for the War Cabinet in London had no intention of seeing repeated the mistakes made after the O'Connor Offensive, and thus losing the recently won gains in Cyrenaica. Tripoli was still to be the main objective for the Eighth Army, and plans for Operation Acrobat—the drive through Tripolitania and linkup with Gymnast somewhere in Tunisia—had already been worked out in some detail. So nothing must be done to decrease Eighth Army strength; but on the other hand nothing, in these new circumstances, could be done for the moment to increase it. The Eighteenth Division now rounding the Cape of Good Hope must, as the Cabinet were sure General Auchinleck would appreciate, be diverted instead to India, as must certain antitank and antiaircraft units and several fighter squadrons.

But in the light of the severe thrashing that Eighth Army had just administered to Panzergruppe Afrika, surely this change of design would be just a temporary disappointment, to be alleviated as quickly as possible and in no way likely to place the Eighth Army in any immediate danger?

With this viewpoint Auchinleck tended to agree, especially as he felt that he now needed a respite to rest and reequip his army, to substitute fresh units for exhausted ones and see that the new divisions in the front areas were properly trained to carry out the next move forward when he felt that the time was ripe. Already he was withdrawing the Seventh Armored Division and regrouping it in Syria and Palestine, and sending up the recently-arrived First Armored to take its place; and both the New Zealanders and South Africans who had played important parts in Operation Crusader were back in the Delta, the only experienced infantry in the forward positions being two brigades of the Fourth Indian Division.

Such thinning out of strength at the front could not have taken place, of course, had not the strength of the Panzergruppe Afrika been so sapped during the recent battles, and to Mr. Churchill's sharp request from Washington for details of the enemy strength that had escaped, Auchinleck replied on January 12, 1942:

> I estimate that not more than one-third of the original German-Italian forces got away round the corner.... These are much disorganised, short of senior officers, short of material, and due to our continuous pressure are tired and certainly not as strong as their total strength, 35,000, might be thought to indicate.

Later on the same day, he sent Churchill another cable:

> Enemy appears to have completed his withdrawal to the Mesa-El Brega-Maaten-Giofa-Aghelia area, and our

troops are in touch with him on his eastern and southern fronts. From our knowledge of his dispositions it seems that his formations and units are numerically weak and that he is ekeing out his scant resources in German troops to stiffen the remnants of the Italian divisions.

It was unfortunate for the British, especially the untried First Armored Division, that General Auchinleck was misreading the situation to a considerable degree.

Rommel had not withdrawn Panzergruppe Afrika—and certainly not the German element of it—because he felt that it had been beaten in the field; in fact, he had been about to mount a powerful counterattack intended to sweep the Eighth Army back to the Egyptian frontier at the very moment that other factors forced him instead to withdraw. Those other factors had been a sudden realization that his supplies of everything from shells for the guns to boots for the infantry —and especially gasoline for his vehicles—were vanishing at an alarming rate, and that the Royal Navy and the Royal Air Force by their continual attacks upon his supply lines had been doing just as much far away from the battlefield to defeat his forces as the Eighth Army had been doing on it.

It had been the attacks upon his army's lines of communication and supply that had caused the retreat, and as, with superlative efficiency, he withdrew the Panzergruppe along them, the lines became shorter—and those of his antagonists longer. He had received forty-five new panzers just before Christmas and another fifty-five during the first days of the New Year, twenty armored cars and a large consignment of fuel. Even more important, he had received some extremely good news.

The onset of the Russian winter had released a considerable number of German aircraft for use elsewhere, and Luftflotte 2 in Southern Italy had recently been substantially reinforced. Moreover, analysis by his own intelligence staff revealed that the Royal Navy had paid a high cost for their contribution to the Crusader Operation, December 1941 proving perhaps the most expensive in their long history. In addition to the losses of the two battleships off the Malayan coast, the aircaft carrier *Ark Royal* and the battleship *Bar-*

ham had been torpedoed in the Mediterranean, and two more battleships, *Valiant* and *Queen Elizabeth* had been immobilized in Alexandria Harbor by Italian frogmen, who blew holes in their hulls with limpet mines so that both now rested uncomfortably on the harbor bottom with their decks and guns only just clear of the water.

In addition, one cruiser had been torpedoed off the Libyan coast and two more sunk in minefields, while one had been withdrawn from the area on orders from the Australian government, who wanted her nearer home. The result was that command of the waters of the Mediterranean and of the air above them had passed in a few days from Allied into Axis hands, and Panzergruppe Afrika was the immediate beneficiary.

Rommel struck early on the morning of January 21 and met with instantaneous success. In two days his panzers practically destroyed the support group of the First Armored Division, and on the morning of January 25 they caught the main bulk of Ritchie's armor and literally drove it from the field. Rommel's intelligence officer, Major von Mellenthin, who watched the attack, later wrote:

> It soon became apparent that the British tank units had no battle experience and they were completely demoralised by the onslaught of the 15th Panzer. At times the pursuit attained a speed of fifteen miles an hour, and the British columns fled madly over the desert in one of the most extraordinary routs in the war. After covering fifty miles in under four hours 15th Panzer reached Msus airfield at 1100, overwhelming numerous supply columns, and capturing twelve aircraft ready to take off. Further exploitation was impossible as the division was out of fuel, but 96 tanks, 38 guns, and 190 lorries were the booty of the day.

Unfortunately for Rommel, however, little or no fuel was captured on that or the following day, and he had thus to forego his early intention of driving across the base of the Cyrenaican Bulge and capturing the entire British and Indian force in the area. Gasoline again was proving the stumbling block to this ambition—and in his perception of this one point, Lt. Gen. Neil Ritchie was right for the first and only time during the battle.

He had been in Cairo when the first German attack was reported, and he arrived in the area the following afternoon to announce that Rommel's advance provided a "God-sent opportunity to hit him really hard when he puts his neck out, as it seems possible that he may already be doing." The possibility that it might have been his own neck that was stuck out did not occur to him, and when the German attack seemed to falter just after the dispersion of the First Armored Division, he announced correctly that it was lack of gasoline that caused it—and incorrectly that Rommel was now splitting his forces.

However, the area commander, Godwin-Austen, could see somewhat further and ordered several swift evacuations—which Ritchie cancelled as soon as he heard about them, precipitating the chaos that inevitably results from "order, counterorder." Inevitably what one shrewd observer of such developments called "the *danse macabre* of military reverse" descended upon the remaining British units, and only determination on the part of the individual commanders saved the bulk of the Indian brigades, though they had to abandon most of their equipment to the gratified pursuers, and only luck saved what few units of the First Armored Division managed to escape.

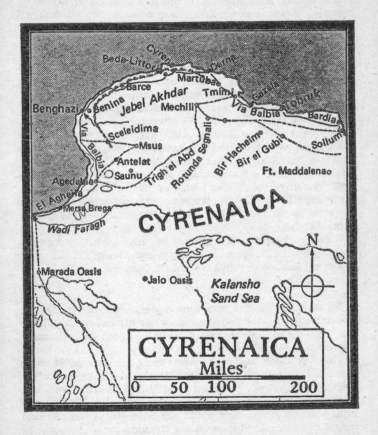

However, now the constraints of Axis High Command intervened to save the British. Mussolini's nerves had been strained to screeching pitch by the news of Rommel's opening attack (for which the German commander had not bothered to obtain clearance, even from Berlin), and as the lines on the map stretched ever further into what Il Duce imagined to be extreme danger—becoming to his horror-struck gaze more and more attenuated as they did so—the orders from Rome followed each other at closer and closer intervals until Rommel's staff felt they were in receipt of a continuous stream of hysteria, demanding an immediate cessation of all military action. This, and a combination of gasoline shortage and the riveting attraction to men who had lived out in the desert for eight months of the delights of life in Benghasi and other towns and villages stacked with abandoned British stores of cigarettes, beer, clean clothes, and tinned fruit, eventually caused a halt in the Panzergruppe advance.

A few of Rommel's reconnaissance squadrons followed close on the heels of the British retreat, picking up stragglers, occasionally fighting briefly with hurriedly formed Indian rearguards, watching the formation of defensive positions south of the Gazala inlet into which the last fugitives of Ritchie's command took refuge. By the beginning of February, the bulk of the Afrika Korps's armor with the infantry of the Ninetieth Light Division were closing up, while the Italian divisions spead out behind and occupied the whole of the Jebel Akhdar.

Weary, weatherworn, thirsty by triumphant, Rommel's forces were back again into Marmarica, with Tobruk once more only thirty-five miles beyond their grasp.

Mr. Churchill's first reactions to this sharp reverse were, not unjustifiably, shock followed by an astonishment bordering on total bewilderment, quickly replaced by sympathy expressed in offers of help.

The first shock had come when the copy of a naval cable came to his attention early in the attack, which suggested that the evacuation of Benghasi was being considered. Mr. Churchill's signal to Auchinleck asking why the British and Indian troops in the port could not hold out as the German troops had at Halfaya Pass during *Crusader,* was answered by one that revealed that Auchinleck was as puzzled as Churchill was by the developing situation. From then on, nothing happened to buttress confidence in the Middle East Command, but Mr. Churchill's spirit of loyalty to a man he greatly admired, however much he disagreed with his strategy and tactics, prevented any immediate vituperation.

But once the movements eastward of the arrows on the maps had stopped at Gazala, many aspects of the developing situation became clearer and thus more critical, and the euphoria that had comforted Mr. Churchill when he returned from Washington evaporated.

The trigger might have been the fall of Singapore on February 15, but developments in Libya did nothing to ease the situation as the fear arose in the prime minister's mind that perhaps in view of this unexpected reverse, American opinion might swing away from North Africa and Europe, and concentrate, after all, on the Pacific. It would not be unreasonable for somebody in Washington to point out that there was not much object in "closing the back door on Rommel" if the front door was open for him to walk through to the Nile.

There was another deeply worrying situation arising in the Mediterranean itself, too, for the last convoy to Malta had been beaten back and the island was not only perilously close to starvation, but also now under attack by Luftlotte 2, which grew heavier every day. This had been due to a sudden switch of Hitler's attention from the Russian to the Mediterranean front, together with his delight at this unexpected success by one of his favorite generals, as a result of which he had decreed the "softening up" of the island preparatory to its possible invasion. Now, with the nearest British airfields back behind Gazala, there was little the Royal Air Force could do to help the embattled island.

The result of these pressures was a cable sent by Mr. Churchill to Auchinleck on February 26:

I have not troubled you much in these difficult days, but I must now ask what are your intentions. According to our figures you have substantial superiority in the air, in armour, and in other forces over the enemy. There seems to be danger that he may gain reinforcements as fast or even faster than you. The supply of Malta is causing us increased anxiety, and anyone can see the magnitude of our disasters in the Far East. Pray let me hear from you. All good wishes.

General Auchinleck's reply covered seven pages, disputed many of the prime minister's figures, stated that there could be no question of a British offensive out of the Gazala line before June 1—and reduced Mr. Churchill to almost incoherent fury.

And little happened during the next three months to assuage it. Every cable that passed between the two men went via Sir Alan Brooke as C.I.G.S., and although those from Auchinleck were couched in the polite usage to which his training had accustomed him, those from Churchill often had to be toned down at Brooke's urgent suggestion. Phrases such as "Soldiers are meant to fight!" and "Armies are not intended to stand about doing nothing!" were excised from some of the prime minister's cables, and the operation of removal led to Brooke's having to withstand quite a number of verbal attacks, although never a blank refusal to make any changes at all.

"The bloody man doesn't seem to care about the fate of Malta," Churchill exploded early in March. "Anyway, we can't settle this by writing letters." He sent a request that Auchinleck come home to Whitehall immediately for discussions, a suggestion for which he had the support of both Brooke and the Chiefs of Staff Committee.

But for reasons that Auchinleck doubtless considered adequate, he refused to come, stating that his presence in Egypt during the retraining of the Eighth Army for the June offensive was essential and that nothing he could say in London would change the import of the messages he was sending from Cairo. It needed all the firmness of a unanimous Chiefs of Staff Committee to prevent Auchinleck's immediate supersession by Lord Gort, at that time governor of Gibraltar. That firmness was more remarkable in view of the fact that Brooke and his colleagues were to a great extent in sympathy with the prime minister's opinion and were themselves coming to the conclusion that Auchinleck was being unnecessarily cautious.

So much did they agree that by early May they were prepared to endorse a cable virtually instructing Auchinleck to submit a plan for an early attack or resign his command, and when that obstacle had been successfully negotiated, they made no alterations to one in which Mr. Churchill, after assuring Auchinleck that he would have their full support in his attack so long as it was not further postponed, included a passage that read:

> I should personally feel greater confidence if you took direct command yourself as in fact you had to do at Sidi Rezegh.

The outcome of this seemingly reasonable request revealed the gap between the view of the romantically minded prime minister in London and that of the professional commander in chief in the Middle East.

To Mr. Churchill the battlefield was all. It was there that glory was to be won by British arms against a famous corps under a brilliant general, and he could not understand how any soldier could hold himself back from the opportunity that the Western Desert now offered.

But to Auchinleck, and to Wavell before him, the desert was nothing but the western flank of a theater of war extending from Afghanistan, via Persia, Iraq, Syria, Palestine, and Egypt to Libya, to which the greatest menace lay on the northeastern front, where huge German armies might swing south and drive down through the Caucasus toward the essential Persian oil fields. To Auchinleck, the battle against Rommel was a tangential affair to be fought by subordinates while he kept his eyes firmly on the main area of threat between the Black Sea and the Caspian. As a result his reply to the prime minister's request was:

> Much as I would like to take command personally in Libya I feel that it would not be the right course to pursue. I have considered the possibility most carefully and have concluded that it would be most difficult for me to keep a right sense of porportion if I became immersed in tactical problems in Libya.

It was this last phrase that stuck in Churchill's gullet. He did not regard the coming conflict with the Afrika Korps as a tactical problem in Libya. He regarded it as a vitally needed victory to provide the Eighth Army with a springboard from which to wrest North Africa from the enemy, unite with the new American armies flooding across the Atlantic, and then attack the main enemy strongholds across the Mediterranean "up through the soft under-belly of Europe." Here was the place for the first step toward ultimate victory to be fought, as soon as possible—and against a worthy foe.

"Rommel! Rommel!" he raved. "What matters but beating Rommel?"

But at least agreement was reached on the date of the attack. By the end of May all preparations would be complete, the whole of the Eighth Army poised and ready for a breakthrough to be followed by a pursuit that would certainly throw Rommel's forces back to El Agheila, soon afterward to Tripoli, perhaps on and into Tunisia. It would be launched on June 1.

There is a much quoted story of a Russian peasant who owned a bear as a pet. One day the bear became ill, so the peasant decided he needed a large pill, and the only way to get it down the bear's throat was by blowing it down through a tube. But the bear blew first.

Panzerarmee Afrika (as it had been lately rechristened) attacked the Gazala line during the night of May 26th–27th. Four Italian infantry divisions closed up to the line in the north while three armored divisions—Italian Ariete, German Fifteenth and Twenty-first Panzer—with the Trieste Motorized Division on the left flank, the Ninetieth Light Division on the right, and Rommel himself in his command vehicle well in front, hooked down around the southern end of the line where the Free French Brigade under Brig. Gen. Pierre Koenig was holding the fortress of Bir Hacheim. The bulk of the German armor flooded on past it and up toward the rear of the center of the line where Rommel believed Ritchie had concentrated not only the bulk of his defending infantry, but also three armored brigades with another just beyond them. All went well during the early part of the day, but nevertheless, he became inceasingly puzzled as the hours passed; by the evening he was seriously worried. It is interesting to analyze why.

His attack had not, in fact, come as a complete surprise to Auchinleck, for again the Ultra organization in England had read enough of Rommel's dispatches to Berlin for them to be able to warn of the intention to attack, and the date, but not the details, as such matters Rommel invariably kept to himself and his immediate staff. Moreover, in order to guard the secret of its existence, Auchinleck was not permitted to reveal the scope and authenticity of the Ultra information to anyone else, and thus could only pass it on to Ritchie in the form of advice and suggestions as to how Ritchie should deploy the forces at his disposal to meet the threat. And invariably Ritchie replied to the effect that he thought the advice excellent and was following it faithfully.

But the Axis powers were not without their own intelligence triumphs, and they had broken the American State Department cipher by which its military representatives reported from the field. Since early 1941 Colonel Bonner Fellers had been in Cairo, and such was his genuine sympathy with the Allied cause that he had been allowed to witness the whole of the Crusader operation from whatever vantage point he requested, and after Pearl Harbor, he was admitted to the innermost circles at G.H.Q.

As such, he attended General Auchinleck's morning conferences with his chief army, navy, and air force staff officers, which, as the day of battle came nearer, went into more and more detail of the deployments of the Eighth Army. Every evening Colonel Fellers sent the details to Washington, and busy interceptors in Bari recorded them, busier interpreters translated them, and their superiors forwarded to Rommel whatever they considered relevant.

So the commander in chief of Panzerarmee Afrika had known more or less how the British commander in chief of the Middle East believed that his commander in the field had deployed the Eighth Army troops behind the Gazala line, and he had been somewhat concerned by the fact that that deployment was well-conceived and exhibiting a sense of concentration of power that had not been much in evidence in previous battles.

But Ritchie, perhaps through sheer misunderstanding or for other reasons that can only be guessed at had in fact *not* followed Auchinleck's suggestions, and instead of concentrating his armor had left it scattered over the desert in comparatively small detachments that Rommel's armor came across unexpectedly, but had little trouble in destroying, capturing, or dispersing. So the main part of the day had gone very well for Rommel.

But by the evening other factors had made themselves

evident. There were, for instance, many more and heavier British antitank guns on the field than he had been led to expect, and they were for the moment quite well handled. But the greatest shock was the appearance of a large number of the new American Grant tanks, equipped with a much heavier gun than had been available to the British before and showing not only more robustness under fire, but a great deal more mechanical dependability. Moreover, Rommel's troops were now coming up against a British battle phenomenon that has frustrated those who fought against them since before Napoleon's day—the ability of junior ranks, from battalion commander down to trooper, to extricate themselves from whatever perils their generals have left them in. Random groups of tank crews, infantry, and gunners from the dispersed formations were coalescing and, out of touch with and thus untrameled by orders from their superiors, were beginning to fight back effectively.

General Grant Tank

"I will not deny," Rommel wrote later, "that I was seriously worried that evening."

Our heavy tank losses were a no good beginning to the battle .... The 90th Light Division under General Kleeman had become separated from the Afrika Korps and was now in a very dangerous position. British motorised groups were streaming through the open gap and hunting down the transport columns which had lost touch with the main body. And on these columns the life of my army depended.

But ultimately, as Napoleon said, in war it is not the men who count, it is *the man;* and Ritchie was no match for Rommel. After a week of fierce fighting in which the battle swayed to and fro, a brigade of British infantry with Indian battalions attached was trapped in what became known as "the caldron," and Ritchie's attempts to relieve them were so inept that Rommel's contempt for his leadership was only equalled by his expressed admiration for the bravery of the men caught there. This was followed by a similar struggle with the Free French down at Bir Hacheim, but when at last that outpost fell, there was nothing for the South African and Northumbrian divisions at the northern end of the Gazala line to do but get out as quickly as they could, which they did with creditable efficiency.

With the main defense line gone, Auchinleck's orders to Ritchie were that Tobruk should be held as the northern strongpoint of another series of defenses stretching back southeastward, and that this line must not be yielded, nor— and this was stressed time and time again—was Tobruk to be invested, a point upon which Churchill, by this time seething with anger and disappointment, was insistent in all his frantic cables to Cairo.

Seven days later Tobruk had not only been invested, it had fallen to an attack from the southeast (all planning had assumed it would come from the southwest) across areas that the Tobruk command thought were mine fields but from which the mines had long been removed for use in the Gazala line. Practically the whole Second South African Division was taken prisoner without firing a shot, for panic had gripped the command staff toward the end of the first day when the extent of the German penetration had been suddenly realized.

Early the following morning a huge white flag was hoisted over the building in which the commanders had taken refuge, and a moan of despair, frustration, and disgust went up from the western half of the fortress area, from thousands of men who were more than willing to fight if only someone present would give them an intelligent lead.

The only aspect of the affair that compared with the ineptitude of the Tobruk command was the fatuity of the messages Ritchie had sent them during the collapse, the last of which read:

Whole of Eighth Army has watched with admiration your gallant fight. You are an example to us all, and I know South Africa will be proud of you.

Enormous booty fell into the hands of the German and Italian forces who captured Tobruk, though to Rommel's fury the gasoline tanks had been set on fire, and some thirty thousand men were marched off toward the prison camps, sick at heart and well aware of the disgrace to British arms.

With Tobruk gone and the desert to the south again littered with groups of men and vehicles making their separate and uncoordinated ways back toward Egypt in the hope of avoiding the marauding German columns, it was quite evident that the next place for an attempt to stem the Axis rush would be at and south of Mersa Matruh, and here Ritchie set about organizing a trap into which he hoped Rommel would thrust his surely overextended and now tired striking force. This in theory was the logical course to pursue, but it overlooked the vital factor of human morale, for if Rommel's men were tired, they were also elated with their triumph and the prospect of life and luxury in Cairo in the near future, while Ritchie's men were angry at the defeats they had just suffered, suspicious of their own neighbors in the defense—whoever they might be—and distrustful of the motives or resolution of the high command.

To Auchinleck, torn between loyalty to his choice of chief subordinate and the reality of the situation, the stream of cables from Whitehall and Washington (for Mr. Churchill had returned there in mid-June) were a constant reminder that the Eighth Army was the only shield between Rommel and first the Delta and then the Persian oilfields. If Ritchie's defense plans now failed and the remainder of that army was destroyed, the Middle East command would have lost the war in six weeks.

On June 25, to the relief of practically everybody when they heard about it, Auchinleck flew up to Maaten Baggush where Ritchie had his headquarters, relieved him of his command, and took it over himself. Immediately he began planning for a withdrawal of the bulk of his troops into the funnel between the coastline and the edge of the Qattara Depression, toward the narrowest part just south of El Alamein.

They were back there by the beginning of July, forming a gradually thickening cork in the neck of a bottle, and Auchinleck was with them to direct the series of battles that has become known as First Alamein. Now the positional advantages were swinging his way, for the Panzerarmee was indeed tired, at the end of ever-lengthening supply lines, and faced with the task of smashing their way by frontal attack through an ever-hardening defense system. Moreover, Auchinleck had never been mesmerized by the prestige of armor and was quite sure that the day of artillery on the field of battle was by no means over.

He therefore centralized this arm under his own control, and during the month that followed, whenever Rommel's panzer and infantry spearheads probed forward in yet another attempt to break through, they found themselves blanketed by drumfire that put Rommel and many of his senior colleagues in mind of the dreadful barrages of the First World War.

By the end of July, both sides were close to exhaustion— the Panzerarmee desperately tired and short of guns, tanks, ammunition, clothes, food, and water, but still to some extent buoyed up by their recent achievements and the still-bright vision of relaxation in the Delta; the Eighth Army close to their depots and thus not so short of equipment or the necessities of life, but dour, sulky, suspicious of orders, contemptuous of the military worth of any formation but their own, unenthusiastic, and still inclined to be distrustful of the leadership. Although they felt that Auchinleck's was a firmer hand than that by which they had lately been led (or misled), few of them had yet seen him or been spoken to by him, and thus had had no opportunity to judge the strength of his personality.

These things matter to all soldiers and especially to those who have suffered a period of defeat.

CHAPTER SEVEN

It had seemed at the time an especially cruel stroke that Mr. Churchill had been with Mr. Roosevelt when the news came through that Tobruk had fallen. He and Sir Alan Brooke were in the president's office when General Marshall entered with a telegram that, after glancing at it, Roosevelt had handed to the prime minister without a word.

"Tobruk has surrendered," it read, "with twenty-five thousand men taken prisoner."

It was, Mr. Churchill wrote later, one of the heaviest blows he was to receive during the war. Not only did it reveal the emptiness of all the assurances he had received from the Middle East Command regarding Tobruk's inviolability, but it cast reflections on the British will to fight. Singapore had surrendered with the loss of eighty-five thousand men only four months before, and now this melancholy repetition brought into question the basic fighting capability of the British army—and at a moment when Churchill had been hoping to persuade his chief allies to follow the British lead in future military operations.

The kindness now extended to him by Mr. Roosevelt and his advisers must stand as a landmark in human generosity and compassion. "What can we do to help?" was the first question the president asked, and with its answer started movements by which three hundred new Sherman tanks and a hundred self-propelled 105-mm. guns were stripped from the American divisions to which they had just been issued, loaded aboard six of the fastest ships that could be found, and sent immediately to the Suez Canal. Few gestures in history have equaled this in faith and loyalty.

Mr. Churchill and his party, which this time included Sir Alan Brooke, had gone to Washington in June to accomplish three tasks: to agree on joint action between the United States and Britain on the development of the atomic bomb; to concert efforts to cut down the Atlantic shipping losses,

105 mm. Self-propelled Gun. Mk. 7

which had risen to appalling heights as the U-boats concentrated off America's eastern seaboard (still spectacularly illuminated); and to try to relight American interest in the proposed North African landings, for, as Mr. Churchill had feared, with the recent rebuffs in the desert, there was a growing body of opinion in Washington that felt that an early drive straight at the heart of Germany across the English Channel would bring the war to an earlier conclusion than any peripheral actions south of the Mediterranean.

Now the fall of Tobruk served to focus attention there, simply by the scale of the catastrophe. From the point of view of military tactics, it could be (and was) argued that Tobruk at that stage of the campaign was not particularly important, but in another aspect it was vitally important, for public opinion from Washington to Berlin was that the fall of the port had been the most telling blow to Allied prestige in three years of war, and in Washington they knew that something must quickly be done about it. The crucial factor would be shipping, and it swung the balance of the argument; if men and arms were to go in worthwhile numbers to the

Middle East, there was just not available the carrying capacity to take similar numbers first to Britian and then to France.

At this point the stature of General George Marshall revealed itself a worthy complement to that of the president. Marshall was a convinced exponent of the direct approach to the task of smashing the Nazi regime, and his favored operation at that time was Operation Sledgehammer, the plan to put six American divisions onto the coast of France before the end of the year.

Now, when he could so easily have used the developments in Africa to buttress his arguments, he turned his back on them and agreed wholeheartedly that the British position n the Middle East must be supported and all possible help sent there. Not only that, but he put even more force into the argument against another inevitable result of the reversals in the desert—the recrudescence of the school of thought that urged the president to turn his back completely on Europe for the moment and concentrate on the Pacific war. Admiral Ernest J. King, commander in chief of the U.S. Navy, was the foremost proponent of this point of view, and in his arguments with the president and General Marshall made no secret of the fact that he looked upon the Japanese as the main enemy, that Hitler could wait, and that the American forces could deal with Europe in due course, even if the British had been beaten and subjugated first.

But fortunately Mr. Roosevelt and General Marshall would not agree, and as both were determined that American troops must be in combat with the Germans before the end of the year, North Africa seemed to be the only practicable theater into which they could be introduced.

The matter had not been completely settled by the time Mr. Churchill and his party were forced by events at home to return, but it was with a certain degree of confidence that he boarded the flying boat at Baltimore on the evening of June 25.

The whole British public and Parliament had been just as distressed as Mr. Churchill by the retreat of the Eighth Army across some five hundred miles of desert during the first six months of the year. The public had expressed its displeasure by returning an opposition candidate at a by-election at

Maldon while Mr. Churchill was in America. The concern of Parliament was indicated when a respected Conservative back-bencher, Sir John Wardlaw Milne, tabled a motion for debate reading:

> That this House, while paying tribute to the heroism and endurance of the Armed Forces of the Crown in circumstances of difficulty, has no confidence in the central direction of the war.

This was a challenge which Mr. Churchill and the government could not ignore, though the prime minister could dismiss its substance upon his arrival in Britain with a curt, "You can't run a war as if you were in a laboratory!" His confidence was well founded, for the motion was defeated—after a comprehensive analysis of the salient points of the conflict to date and a magnificent call to action in his own closing speech—by 475 votes to 25.

But it had taken up valuable time, time that need not have been wasted if the Eighth Army had advanced instead of retreated at Gazala; if, in Mr. Churchill's opinion, Auchinleck had been in sole command from the beginning.

Even after the Parliamentary success, there were other matters to occupy Churchill's attention, for the great German drive in Russia toward the Don and the Caucasus had begun, a convoy had been practically destroyed by U-boats en route to Murmansk, and Stalin's demands for a second front had grown so strident that opinion in Washington was again veering back toward the idea of an immediate cross-Channel operation. On July 18, General Marshall, Admiral King, and Mr. Hopkins arrived in London, and once again the arguments for and against Operation Sledgehammer were fought over.

In these, Sir Alan Brooke was the chief British spokesman, parrying American enthusiasm and optimistic certainty with cold, probing logic.

Where were these six American divisions so well-trained that they could undertake this highly complicated operation by September? Where were the landing craft to take them across the Channel? As neither the weather nor tidal condition would allow such an operation after mid-September, the six divisions must not only be very quickly ashore but equally quickly expanding their bridgehead so that the sea was beyond Luftwaffe fighter range, or they could not be fed and maintained during the immediately succeeding months; was General Marshal sure that this was possible? How would the divisions be maintained through the January and February gales, let alone those to be expected in March?

Above all, upon what grounds did the American commanders base their belief that the German Wehrmacht, its morale still high, its faith in German victory still undimmed, would be unable to bring up sufficient force to throw the American divisions back into the sea—if indeed, it ever allowed them to land? And after four days of such grueling interrogation, General Marshall capitulated, cabled Washington, and Mr. Roosevelt informed the prime minister that it had been agreed that no Operation Sledgehammer could take place in 1942. Instead, all American planning would now be directed toward an Anglo-American landing in North Africa.

Overjoyed, Mr. Churchill rechristened the operation Torch, agreed that the supreme commander should be Lt. Gen. Eisenhower with a combined Anglo-American staff, that the deputy commander should be Lt. Gen. Sir Harold Alexander, and that the British task force should be commanded by the difficult, opinionated but undoubtedly talented Lt. Gen. Sir Bernard Law Montgomery.

Now, at last, the prime minister could redirect his attention to the only theater where armies of the Western Alliance were in direct contact with the enemy. He must go out and see for himself what had gone wrong in the Middle East.

Mr. Churchill had already agreed that Sir Alan Brooke should visit the Delta, but in view of the danger areas they would both be flying over, they went by different routes—Sir Alan via Gibraltar and Malta, Churchill in an American Liberator that also stopped at Gibraltar but then made a long sweep south across the Sahara to reach the Nile at Beni Suef, then flew north to Cairo. By the early morning of August 3, Churchill was installed in an air-conditioned room in the British embassy, exhilarated to be on the spot, especially since at Gibraltar he had received a cable from Auchinleck indicating that he intended no further offensive action in the desert until mid-September.

This would not do at all. Torch was scheduled for the end of October, and by that time Rommel must have been pushed out of Egypt, and preferably past Benghasi as well, if not back to Tripoli, thus so impressing French opinion that they would not oppose too fiercely the Anglo-American landings in Algeria and Morocco.

At six o'clock that evening the first conference was held at which General Auchinleck, who had come back from the front especially for it, reported upon the exact situation and condition of the Eighth Army and then went on to explain the dangers that threatened other flanks of his command and the measures he had taken to meet them. At dinner Mr. Churchill remained unusually silent, obviously thinking matters over, but at midnight he sent for Sir Alan Brooke for further discussions.

Sir Alan and the Chiefs of Staff were insistent that the place for the commander in chief was in Cairo; therefore, another competent and energetic general must be appointed to command the army at the front. It seemed to Mr. Churchill from all that he had heard that there was just such a general already present—Lt. Gen. H. E. "Strafer" Gott, a veteran of desert warfare who was now commanding XIII Corps and who, to use Churchill's words, "had not earned the title Strafer for nothing."

It was not a choice that immediately appealed to Sir Alan. Recent experience as typified by the Ritchie appointment (and Sir Alan was "devoted to Neil," who had been his chief of staff in France) suggested that too quickly accelerated promotion might hold the seeds of unfortunate consequence, and Gott's promotions had been very quick indeed. During the O'Connor Offensive he had been a brigadier commanding the support group of the Seventh Armored Division, during Crusader he had commanded the division itself as a major general, and he had received his latest promotion just before the Gazala battles. Although no one was for a moment suggesting that he was in any way responsible for the flood of disasters since then, there had not been time to examine the reports in sufficient detail to be sure that he had, in fact, risen to the full heights that his rank demanded.

Undoubtedly he was a brave and thoroughly professional soldier, and no one's name stood higher than his throughout the army as a whole, but he had been in the desert for a very long time, all the appointments he had held had made great demands upon him, and it would be astonishing if he were not in need of a rest, preferably at home and in a cooler climate, with probably a complete change of scene afterward. Why not Montgomery?

But Churchill insisted that Gott was present there and now and knew the Eighth Army, whereas Montgomery was in England, would take time to come out, and then have to get to know a totally new command. On the other hand, why didn't Brooke take over out here as commander in chief and then choose whomever he liked to command at the front?

It was an enormous temptation, but Sir Alan took only a few minutes to turn it down. For one thing, he could not bear the idea that Auchinleck, for whom he had the greatest respect and admiration, would feel that he had come out to Egypt to supersede him; but a second reason was that in eight months he had learned some of the techniques by which his volatile master could be to some extent controlled, and he felt that he could best serve the country by remaining in his arduous and often highly uncomfortable post by Churchill's side.

It was two o'clock before the two men got to bed, so no one saw Mr. Churchill until lunchtime (he was never an early riser if he could help it), but the evening meeting was composed of the most authoritative personalities in the area —Brooke, Auchinleck, Wavell, who had flown in from Delhi, Admiral Harwood and Air Marshal Tedder, and the minister of state for the Middle East, Mr. Richard Casey. It was, in one vital respect, a repeat of the meetings with Auchinleck of the previous year in London, for no matter what arguments Mr. Churchill produced, whatever anyone else around the table suggested, Auchinleck did not budge an inch from his declaration that the Eighth Army could not launch another major offensive for at least six weeks.

Mr. Churchill was very irritated and again talked into the night with Brooke, who in turn again pressed the choice of Montgomery to command the army, for Brooke's inquiries during the day had confirmed his suspicion that Gott was indeed tired. At this, Churchill became somewhat impatient, repeated his arguments that Montgomery was in England while Gott was on the spot, and then veered off on to the old complaint of the underemployment of Maitland Wilson.

Fortunately for Brooke, visits to the front were scheduled for the following day, and even Mr. Churchill would have to be up by five o'clock, so they were in bed by one. But the unfortunate C.I.G.S. did note that as a fifty-nine-year-old professional soldier he was feeling the strain of the last four days of travel, heat, and argument, yet the sixty-eight-year-old prime minister seemed in his element.

They flew up to Burg el Arab the following morning, drove across the desert, and breakfasted at Auchinleck's headquarter mess, a wire cage, which instead of keeping the flies out trapped them inside so that they rose in a buzzing cloud whenever disturbed, and thoroughly put all the visitors off their food. It may have been Auchinleck's intention to let the prime minister see the conditions in which he and his men lived, but the effect was to put him into a bad, not an understanding, mood. An hour-long session with Auchinleck and his chief of staff, Lt. Gen. Eric Dorman-Smith, followed in the hot and uncomfortable command caravan, during which the prime minister could make no headway with his arguments against either of them, and he departed very displeased. From there he went for the lunchtime engagement with the Air Force commanders at their advanced headquarters, taking with him General Gott and thus upsetting Auchinleck's arrangements for an afternoon conference with his corps commanders.

Churchill was impressed by Gott. The famous desert warrior did not appear tired to him (he was, in fact, infected by the prime minister's own vitality and enthusiasm), and although he admitted he would like some leave in England, he would certainly accept command of the army if Mr. Churchill felt he could fill the post satisfactorily.

The reception at RAF headquarters improved the occasion. Here was no wire cage full of flies, here was an open beach cooled by sea breezes, white table linen, gleaming silver, brandy in cut glasses, and an excellent lunch sent out from Shepheards Hotel. Above all, here were men who had not suffered a series of reverses, who were members of a young service not bound by old traditions, who were prepared to say what was in their minds without thought of breaking convention. No record of what exactly was said seems to have been kept, but some idea was provided many years later when Lord Tedder's memoirs were published, including letters written home at about this time.

The difference between those Army meetings and (our own) meetings is the difference between a funeral breakfast and a wedding breakfast. There's no life about them. Too many old men and "nice chaps." As Auck. remarked to me, the Army is suffering from "good fellows."
I wish he (Auchinleck) was a better judge of character. . . . I also wish he had the ability to inspire the army here.

Mr. Churchill had a great deal to think about on his way home and was very quiet during the dinner that followed.

But the following morning he burst into Sir Alan Brooke's bedroom while the latter was still dressing, with the announcement that he had found the solution to all the problems and would discuss them over breakfast.

The main objection that he, Churchill, had to Auchinleck's attitude was his concentration on the northern front instead of the desert—and perhaps it was justified; the oil fields were vital to Britain's war effort and possibly more important than Egypt. But Rommel must be beaten—and soon.

Therefore, Auchinleck must be allowed to concentrate where his interest lay, and another commander in chief appointed to take over the battlefield area, thus the huge Middle East Command would be split in two. Westward from the Suez Canal would constitute a separate theater—say, Near East—and the title Middle East would now apply to the area east of the Canal, still commanded by Auchinleck with whomever he chose as subordinate commander for the forces in the field. Why didn't Brooke take over as commander in chief in Cairo, and as he was so keen on Montgomery, then with Montgomery commanding the Eighth Army?

This did not look practical to Brooke, first because he still felt it his duty to remain by Churchill's side, second because he felt that the Suez Canal would be an impossible dividing line. The day's wrangling left Churchill annoyed and petulant, and in the compromise that was eventually worked out and cabled to Whitehall for agreement, some of the annoyance was vented on subordinate heads. General Auchinleck was to be offered the post of commander in chief of the new Middle East Command, Alexander to relinquish his post with Torch and become commander in chief of the new Near East

Command. Montgomery would move up to take Alexander's place as deputy commander of Torch, and Gott would take over Eighth Army. Lieutenant Generals Corbett, Ramsden, and Dorman-Smith would be relieved of their commands.

The Eighth Army would need two new corps commanders (and the commander in chief would need a new chief of staff), but those appointments could be decided in due course.

But then Fate took a hand. Two days later, as the first changes were taking place and Gott was flying back from the front to take up the reins of his new command, the airplane in which he was traveling was shot down by marauding Luftwaffe fighters. He was not hurt at the time, but went back into the plane to help with a man who had been wounded; one plane returned, again shot at the wreck, and Gott was killed instantly.

That afternoon a cable was sent to Whitehall asking that General Montgomery be sent out immediately by special aircraft to take over command of the Eighth Army, under General Alexander.

Nobody, up to that moment, had ever called Montgomery a nice chap or a good fellow; he would probably have been very annoyed if they had.

Most of the changeovers took place with dignity and a minimum of fuss. One of Churchill's staff ("feeling as if I were about to murder an unsuspecting friend") took a letter out to Auchinleck telling him of the decision to relieve him of his present command and offering him the new position east of Suez. Having read it with typical impassivity, Auchinleck said he doubted if he could accept the offer, for a number of reasons. These he outlined in a "bleak but impeccable interview" with Churchill on August 9, the chief reason being that it would all smack too much in the public eye of a sinecure being found for an unsuccessful general—a policy he would disapprove of for anyone else, so could not countenance for himself.

That day Alexander arrived and arranged the date for his assumption of command with all the enormous charm and tact for which he was well known, making the interview with Auchinleck and his staff as easy as possible. But on August 12 Montgomery arrived, and the atmosphere became much less cordial. As Alexander was not to take over for another three days, it was to Auchinleck that Montgomery had first to report, and it was a prickly, thoroughly uncomfortable affair in which Montgomery made no attempt to disguise his attitude of thinly veiled contempt for all military command as exercised in the area to date; he then talked at some length to the deputy chief of the General Staff at Cairo headquarters, Brigadier John Harding with whom he had worked before, then arranged to meet another old acquaintance, Brigadier Francis de Guingand, who was at that time Auchinleck's senior staff officer at the front.

The two had a long talk on the way out to Burg el Arab and then on toward El Alamein, and of it de Guingand was later to write:

> It was extraordinary how he had spotted most of the weaknesses even before his arrival. And he gave out his ideas to a gathering of all the Headquarters Staff officers that very evening. . . . That address by Montgomery will remain one of my most vivid recollections. . . . We all felt that a cool and refreshing breeze had come to relieve the oppressive and stagnant atmosphere.

A number of points that Montgomery made in that talk he was going to repeat many times afterwards, and they became fundamental rules for conduct in all the armies to come under his command. One of them was that there was to be no more questioning or even discussion of orders that came down from the top, and all bellyaching was to stop; orders were directives for action, not subjects for debate. Another point that he stressed (and thus gained the instant support of, among others, Maj. Gen. Sir Bernard Freyberg, commanding the New Zealanders) was that in the future, divisions would fight as divisions, and not be split up into smaller battle groups or other secondary formations, whatever they might be called.

But above all, there would be no more retreat. "If we cannot stay here alive, then let us stay here dead!" No one who heard Montgomery say it believed for one second that he excluded himself from that commitment. Amid the torrent of criticism that during his life Montgomery called down upon his own head, there was never any questioning of his physical courage.

But that evening he did take one last opportunity to show his personal disinclination to obey orders, at any rate from

General Auchinleck. Dismissing General Ramsden, who had been appointed temporary commander of the Eighth Army, back to his corps, Montgomery sent a cable to Cairo Headquarters ordering the immediate destruction of all plans for withdrawal and announced his intention to take command immediately and not wait until the official date of his appointment in two days' time. That night he went to sleep with an insubordinate smile on his face; he was issuing orders to an army that someone else thought he commanded.

One of the orders he had issued had immediate results. He had looked briefly at the plans drawn up by Auchinleck and Dorman-Smith for the next battle—it was expected that Rommel would soon make a further attempt to break through to the Delta—and he decided to plan not for a mobile battle but for one in which the Eighth Army would form a solid mass against which Rommel must throw his Panzerarmee and perhaps dash it to pieces in the attempt; and for this Montgomery needed another infantry division. The Forty-fourth Division had recently arrived in the Delta, and that very first evening de Guingand was instructed to ring Cairo and order its immediate dispatch to the front. But the staff, not surprisingly, queried the authority and maintained that the division was still unacclimatized and could not move up until the end of the month.

Montgomery then rang Harding, who forwarded his request first to Auchinleck and then to Alexander.

"Is that what Monty wants?" asked Alexander when the request reached him.

"Yes."

"Then do it!"

The bulk of the division was in place within two days and the rest within three, and they were to play a vital part in the battle to come. But first, there was another aspect of the Eighth Army's fitness for battle to be dealt with.

Montgomery never pretended that he did not enjoy the manner in which he made himself known to the troops, excited their enthusiasm, and thoroughly imprinted his own personality upon his command—and the fact of his enjoyment should not obscure the necessity for the process. For far too long the troops had endured the filth and hardship of desert life and the death and destruction of battle, without ever seeing or hearing from the men in command, the men in whose hands their lives and fortunes were held.

Now the topmost man, the commander himself, was coming out to see them all, to talk to them, sometimes to listen to them but mostly to tell them what his plans were, and the part they each had to play in them. Perhaps what most impressed them at first was that he actually arrived on time and didn't keep them standing about for hours in the blazing sun; that, and the fact that he dressed so that he became instantly recognizable.

Gone very quickly were the polished buttons on the smooth barathea, gone the battle dress and even the uniform khaki drill; soon he was wearing the suede boots, the corduroy slacks, the open-necked shirt, and the pullover that had long been acceptable desert wear. Next went the peaked and red-banded cap in which he had arrived. One of the first formations he visited was the Australian division, and from them he sequestered one of their slouch hats and an Australian sunburst badge to go with it. Every formation he visited for some time afterward contributed another hat badge until the high crown was dotted with the metal emblems.

But he was just as aware of his appearance as any other prima donna, and the large hat tended to show up the sharpness of his features and his rather foxy look. So the big hat was replaced by the black beret and just two badges—Royal Tank Corps and general staff—much to the annoyance of several cavalry officers who felt that as a mere infantryman, their commander had no right to their colored hat.

The visits went on, the talks, and the sudden appearances. Although some officers might scoff and the more conventional ones register shock and—if they fell foul of his drive for greater efficiency and were promptly sacked—anger; and although quite a large number of the troops, grown cynical of all army command, listened to his diatribes and promises with scepticism and commented with sarcasm, a new spirit did begin to spread through the army. It was not yet one of confidence, but it was one of hope; and there was one greatly significant development. The officers and men of the Eighth Army stopped talking about Rommel as though he were the only general in North Africa.

Churchill and Brooke arrived back on August 17. (They had gone on from Cairo to Moscow, and there the prime minister had taken on the task of telling Stalin in person that there would be no second front in 1942, but that large-scale offensives were planned at both ends of the North African theater. M. Stalin had in the end proved unexpectedly agreeable.) Two days later, both Churchill and Brooke went again into the desert, where they stayed in considerable comfort in the new Eighth Army headquarters by the sea. Before dinner Montgomery gave them a report on the developments since their departure and on his interpretation of Rommel's situation, the steps he thought the German general would take, and those he would himself take to thwart them. Of the address Brooke later wrote:

> Monty's performance that evening was one of the highlights of his military career. . . . I knew my Monty pretty well by then, but I must confess that I was dumbfounded by the rapidity with which he had grasped the essentials, the clarity of his plans, and above all, his unbounded self-confidence—a self-confidence with which he inspired all those that he came into contact with.

According to Montgomery, Rommel would attack in the south, just below the Alam Halfa Ridge upon which Montgomery had massed the Forty-fourth Division and several tank brigades. He would attack during the early morning of August 31, and the German armor that got safely through the mine fields would then find itself under a combination of RAF bombing and gunfire—the latter from massed artillery and tanks immobile in hull-down positions. This would stop the Germans as though they had run into a wall. They would then be forced inexorably to retreat to their original line, and Montgomery would keep up the pressure; but under no circumstances would the British armor be allowed to charge forward in their usual dashing style, as Montgomery intended to hoard his tanks for the future.

Only the persuasion of Brooke and the promptings of a reluctant conscience took the prime minister home by August 24, but on the night of the battle and for the next two days, Downing Street was in a fever of excitement, only relaxed on the evening of September 3 when Ultra intercepted and translated Rommel's cable to Berlin announcing that he was calling off the operation and withdrawing from what had become for his armor and most experienced men nothing but a deathtrap.

Montgomery had done what he had said he would—and done it on time. When would he himself attack, pushing Rommel and his Panzerarmee out of Egypt, across Tripolitania, and eventually out of North Africa altogether?

CHAPTER EIGHT

Some years after the war Mr. Churchill was asked which time had been for him the most anxious, and he answered without hesitation, "September and October, 1942." He had shown little sign then of the strain under which he was laboring, presenting to the world an appearance of cheerful, even gay, confidence, but quite undoubtedly those two months appeared to him, and indeed to many other people in Britain, very dark indeed.

Rommel may have been stopped at Alam Halfa, but for how long? In any case, wars are not won by just stopping the enemy; would the new combination in the Middle East really prove effective enough not only to win a victory clear and apparent at the time, but also decisive enough for the gains to be held and then exploited? The catalog of disasters to British arms in the desert ever since the arrival of the Germans, especially during the last three months, gave little real promise of justifiable hope for the immediate future, and even though the government might have won that vote of confidence in Parliament, there was now a growing mood throughout the country, which was beginning to question the whole direction and control of the war effort.

Articles had already appeared in the popular press reflecting this attitude, including one in the Labour *Tribune* entitled "Why Churchill?" which was nothing but a savage personal attack on him. Inside the Cabinet itself was a continual threat from Sir Stafford Cripps, leader of the House of Commons, to resign in protest at what he saw as inefficiency and waste of effort throughout the government. It was, of course, too much to expect Churchill and Cripps to agree on any subject (except that Hitler should be defeated) for they disagreed on practically everything. Cripps was an austere, dogmatic Socialist who neither smoked tobacco nor drank alcohol, ate very sparingly and usually from a vegetarian diet, took a lawyer's view of every subject, and was totally opposed to anything that smacked of romanticism, intuition, imagination, or any concept that could not be spelled out in precise, formal terms. Only the fact that the two men needed little personal contact in pursuit of their respective duties had avoided a major row before this, but now the long run of defeats had affected Cripps to the extent that he felt he must make a public protest.

But fortunately the two men shared one quality, a strong sense of duty, and when appealed to, Cripps agreed to postpone his resignation until after the next battle in the desert. When would that be?

Even with such pressures to raise the temperature of his own ever-ardent nature, Mr. Churchill realized it would be both unfair and imprudent to harass Alexander or Montgomery regarding the opening of the new offensive before the noise of Alam Halfa had died down. And in any case, Operation Torch was to take place at a date bearing at least some relation to the Eighth Army's next move, and there were innumerable problems to be solved in that regard—one of which became suddenly acute even before Alam Halfa was fought.

Mr. Churchill had already established very friendly relations with the two senior American generals in England, Lt. Gen. Dwight D. Eisenhower and Maj. Gen. Mark Clark. Indeed, they usually lunched with him every Tuesday, and both were frequent visitors at Chequers. Since the end of July, they had both been fully engaged in the planning for Torch—perhaps one of the complex operations in the whole history of war to that date.

Its strategic aim was to put Allied forces ashore on the coast of North Africa in such strength and at such locations that they could reach and occupy the main centers of Bizerta and Tunis before the enemy, whose Sicilian bases were less than three hundred miles away. Those Allied forces had to cross either four thousand miles of ocean from the east coast of America or two thousand miles from Scotland, and land either on the west coast of Africa outside the Straits of Gibraltar—probably at Casablanca—or inside the Mediterranean and thus be in danger of strangulation if Axis forces successfully closed the Straits.

The distance from Casablanca to Tunis was 1,274 miles, the road system was rudimentary and neither sufficiently

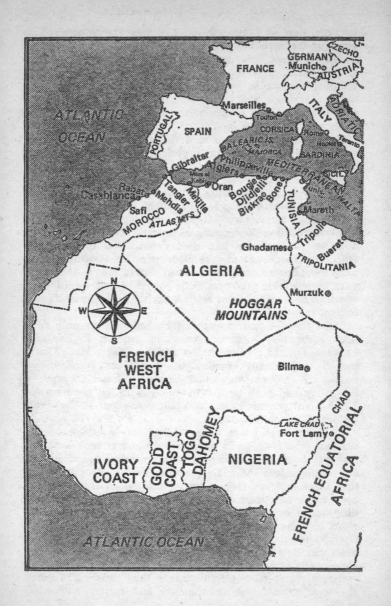

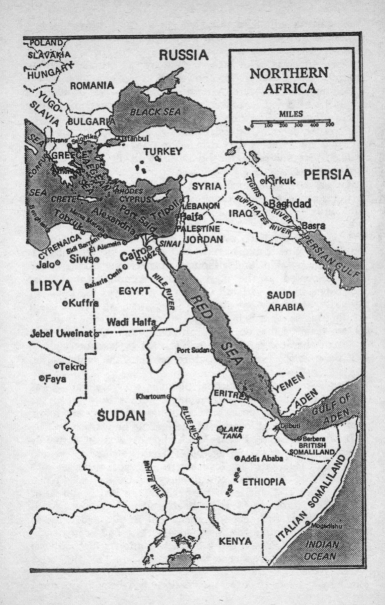

well-constructed nor diverse enough to carry heavy military traffic, while only one narrow gauge and somewhat dilapidated railway line wound its uncertain way between the various towns and ports. The area covered by the original directive addressed to General Eisenhower exceeded a million square miles and covered three countries whose native populations could be assumed to object to the sudden incursion of large numbers of heavily armed foreigners. Moreover, their rulers, the French colonial administrators, received their orders from Vichy France and if they decided to obey them to the letter, would therefore resist the operation with all the force they could muster.

Other, less wide-ranging but equally crucial tactical and administrative factors complicated the problem twenty-fold. Obviously there was a minimum strength to be put ashore, which if lessened would render the operation pointless. But every man, every tank, every gun, shell, and bullet, and every pint of gasoline would have to be carried to the disembarkation point by ship, and although the necessary tonnage had been allocated at the start of the planning, the U-boat campaign in the Atlantic was rising to a new pitch of intensity, and every day shipping losses rose. Again and again loading tables were being redrafted in the light of cargo and escort vessels allocated to Torch being sunk. Other ships of different characteristics were being listed to take their place; often they were torpedoed before reaching the embarkation ports.

And even while the tactical planning and replanning was taking place, political disagreements were arising as to the operation's main purpose, the constitution of the assault force, and the number and location of the landing points.

It was early agreed that Torch should be given a mainly American aspect, as the age-old French hostility to Britain had been exacerbated by British refusal to accept defeat with France in 1940, by the Royal Navy attack on the French fleet at Mers el Kebir the same year, by the British defeat of the French forces in Syria in 1941, and perhaps most of all by the support and encouragement that Britain had given to the traitor de Gaulle and his followers, who had brought disgrace upon the French army by their mutinous disobedience of the orders to surrender to the Germans.

But America's traditional ties with Republican France, aided by the fact that formal relations had been maintained with Vichy and that since 1940 several shiploads of food and clothing had been sent from America to North Africa for distribution made it likely that French resistance to military forces carrying the Stars and Stripes would not be so fierce. Perhaps it would only be nominal, perhaps nonexistent; and in this regard, the chief American consul, Mr. Robert Murphy, was already carefully sounding out opinion among some of the senior military and civilian officials.

But if the bulk of the landing forces was to be American, the greater part of the naval contribution would have to be British, and so also must be the main air cover, at least during the landing operations. Aircraft carriers were in very short supply, and the only shore base from which aircraft could operate was Gibraltar, where the entire headquarter organization must be set up. Despite its appearance, therefore, the operation would have to be a joint Anglo-American one, its controlling staff totally integrated, using the same technical terms despite differences in linguistics, acting in complete sympathy as though they were not only of the same nation, but also of the same service. It is a tribute to General Eisenhower's sense of purpose, as well as his personal charm, that long before the time came to leave for Gibraltar, he had welded together just such an organization in London.

But even Eisenhower's personality could not reach across the Atlantic. In London the planning staff had listened to the Royal Naval point of view, which held that surf conditions west of the Straits were such that on only one day in five would landings be possible at Casablanca but that a combination of air cover from Gibraltar and Royal Naval expertise and experience inside the Mediterranean would be sufficient to guarantee—as far as any operation of war could be guaranteed—the safety of passage of the convoys to landing places east of the Straits and thus nearer to the ultimate targets in Tunisia. Oran, Algiers, and Bône were thus chosen as first objectives and landing places.

So it was with consternation that Eisenhower and Clark received on August 25 a cable from Washington announcing that the American Chiefs of Staff considerd the planned scope for Torch too large for the military force available, that the prime and possibly only landing must be at Casablanca in order to secure a firm and unthreatened base, and that Oran was the furthest point inside the Mediterranean that could be attempted. It was, as Mr. Churchill afterward described it, a bombshell to the American generals then, and to himself and the British planners when it was revealed to them six days later—during the opening hours of Alam Halfa.

Then began what Eisenhower later described as the Great Transatlantic Essay Competition.

It seems probable that the main cause of the disagreement was the American suspicion of British motives, for even the demonstrable fact that the opening of the Mediterranean route to the Far East would save something like a million tons of Allied shipping a year seemed to carry little weight in Washington. General Marshall was still doubtful of the value of any strategy that did not drive straight at Berlin—though he now accepted that landings on the Channel coast would be impossible in 1942—and seems to have felt vaguely that Churchill's and Brooke's concentration on a Mediterranean strategy was at best a relic of Britain's imperialist past, at worst a symptom of new colonial ambitions with which he and the American people would be strongly antipathetic.

But the main factor in everyone's argument was still shipping. Admiral King had launched the opening phase of his Pacific strategy in August with attacks at Guadalcanal and Tulagi, and if the concept was both brave and perceptive, it was also expensive. Within a few days four United States cruisers had been sunk, and during the weeks that followed both merchant and fighting navies paid a high price for the victory that was undoubtedly won there. But shipping pulled by events into the Pacific would not be available for Torch.

The picture was similar elsewhere, for Hitler had now become an enthusiast for the U-boat campaign, and over a hundred were operating in the Atlantic. Although the convoy system had at last been introduced off the American eastern seaboard, the "wolf packs" were still attacking fiercely, with some success, and indeed with great daring, for two Canadian destroyers were torpedoed and sunk in the Gulf of St. Lawrence itself. Moreover, two Royal Naval destroyers and a cruiser were sunk off Tobruk while covering an abortive commando raid, while an important convoy to Murmansk, although it avoided the near annihilation of the ill-fated P.Q. 17 in June, still lost a third of its strength despite a naval deployment for its protection of seventy-seven ships!

And it was the situation in Russia that caused Mr. Churchill the gravest concern and the deepest embarrassment. By the end of August the panzers were driving down into the

Caucasus to reach the oil fields at Grozny, Stalingrad was already invested, and the Black Sea naval port of Novorossisk was under threat. Soon Hitler would order his armies to swing north for the gigantic onslaught on Stalingrad—and at this critical moment the demands for Torch made it quite evident that no more shipping could be spared for Russian convoys until it was successfully completed—by which time the winter weather might have rendered them impracticable for many months! What would Stalin's reaction be in the face not only of attacks of his enemies, but of the apparent failure to help of his allies?

This was the aspect of affairs that most worried Mr. Churchill. At Moscow he had placated the Russian dictator with assurances that in place of an immediate second front in Europe, Britian's air forces would pound German cities to dust, that huge American armies would invade North Africa and drive eastward through Tunisia toward Tripoli, while the Eighth Army in its turn smashed the Axis forces under General Rommel and drove the remnants westward until the two jaws of the vice met to crush all traces of Axis power on the Dark Continent out of existence. This would be followed by an early asault on Sicily and perhaps the opening of a second front in Italy.

Now much of this seemed doubtful. The demands on Bomber Command from every quarter—from the admiralty for attacks on the U-boat pens along the Normandy coast or for attacks on the German battleships on the Norwegian fjords, from the Torch planners for the destruction of Italian factories—all combined to keep the skies above the German heartland comparatively empty, the supply trains feeding the Panzerarmees running smoothly. As for the Mediterranean theater, the attack on North Africa was now apparently to be confined to the two outermost landing places, one at Casablanca, a thousand miles from its objective, and the other at Oran, over six hundred; and in the opinion of Mr. Churchill's naval advisers, landings could only take place on the Casablanca beaches one day in five!

It was a time for Draconian measures, for vital decisions to be taken at the top, so an aircraft was kept available at all hours of the day and night to whisk the prime minister back to Washington in case the flow of cables revealed the imminence of a major row. At this point Sir Charles Wilson warned Sir Alan Brooke that such a trip in conditions of such general strain might have disastrous consequences. Could Sir Alan go on his own?

As it happened, this particular crisis was resolved at the last moment by President Roosevelt, who insisted upon a compromise. Whatever the opinion of his military advisers, he wanted American troops in action as soon as possible, and landing them a thousand miles from the nearest German or Italian armies seemed unlikely to bring this about. American-built landing craft earmarked for Casablanca must be made available for use at Algiers in such quantities that 10,000 troops would be put ashore there—only the leading formations being American, the main mass British, who would then drive eastward into Tunisia with the less-experienced Americans following immediately behind. Casablanca, Oran, and Algiers were confirmed as landing places.

There was a jubilant exchange of cables between Downing Street and the White House, a flurry of action and excitement in Whitehall as the news spread that firm decisions had at last been made, and an announcement by General Eisenhower that he could now give a firm date for the landings—November 8, 1942.

Undoubtedly this was another shock to Mr. Churchill, who wanted Torch to take place at the latest in October, but he obviously had not the authority over the American generals that he had over the British, and could not press them unduly. Not that there would have been much point. Generals Eisenhower and Clark with their planning staffs were now grappling with the problems of moving an assault force of 90,000 men to be followed quickly by 200,000 more, with all their supplies and weapons, across 2,000 miles of sea from Britain and 4,000 from America, all in the face of submarines and air attack, and landing them on neutral territory in which the Allies did not control a single port or airstrip. The assault may or may not be resisted by 200,000 French troops supported by an air force of some 500 aircraft and a naval force that, however it might feel toward one half of the invaders, was bitterly hostile to the other half, whose ships were carrying the bulk of the men and supplies. Aircraft from at most three carriers and from the crowded airstrip on Gibraltar, 500 miles from Algiers, was all that would be available to cover the initial landings. In order to obtain more convenient air covers for future operations, however, paratroops would be flown across 1,200 miles of Occupied France to drop ahead of the seaborne forces.

With such problems to deal with, the American generals could do without extra exacerbation from the British prime minister, whatever the degree of friendliness in their personal relations. Mr. Churchill was now to find that the two most implicated British generals were equally impervious to his promptings for early action.

One of the main causes of Mr. Churchill's dissatisfaction with General Auchinleck at the end had been the latter's inflexible determination not to launch the Eighth Army into attack before mid-September. But when on September 15 the prime minister inquired as to General Alexander's immediate intentions, the reply was that the impending battle would require a full moon so that the infantry would be able to clear paths through the enemy mine fields; that General Montgomery's army would not be sufficiently well-trained for the September moon but that he would guarantee victory in October; and if Mr. Churchill or anyone else wanted the Eighth Army to attack before that date, they would have to find someone else to put in command!

It was, as Montgomery was afterward to admit, pure blackmail on his part—but blackmail backed up by the Alam Halfa success and his growing confidence and control of the army. To Mr. Churchill's frustration it quickly became evident that there was nothing to do but accept the situation. Sir Alan Brooke and the Chiefs of Staff supported the Middle East generals, and all the prime minister could do was to call for the details of Montgomery's plans (which were very reluctantly released to him and then only in general terms) and accept the basic prognosis—three days for the break-in, seven days to the break-out, and 10,000 casualties.

But already there seemed to be a shift in power, a diminution of Churchill's authority, of his ability to command or even influence events. He had no power at all of appointment or dismissal over two of the generals planning a major assault on the enemy. And by a twist of irony, he would only wield such power as he had exercised in the past over his generals if Alexander and Montgomery's efforts against Rommel and his Panzerarmee failed; in which case it was highly likely that the British public would demand his own replacement at Downing Street.

There seemed no end to the strains to be imposed upon him, for having been forced to accept that neither of the desert offensives would be launched as early as he had promised Stalin, he received at the beginning of October a cable from the Russian dictator reporting the fall of Novorossisk and an ominous deterioration of the entire military situation on the eastern front. Demands had already been sent to Washington from Moscow for a supply of at least five hundred aircraft and eight thousand tanks, and Stalin and the Russian people expected Britain to supply not only the necessary merchant shipping, but also enough of her naval strength to insure its safe delivery.

Desperately, Churchill wracked his mind and plagued his advisers for some sop to throw to the hard pressed, ruthless men in the Kremlin and in desperation returned to a project he had frequently suggested before—another invasion of Norway with the object of both attracting German strength away from the Russian front and securing a base in the north from which the Murmansk convoys could be protected. He met as usual a blank wall of opposition against which he could make no headway at all. The Chiefs of Staff were unanimous that even under the best of conditions the project would be disastrous; in the present circumstances an attempt

P-39 Bell Aircobra

to launch even the first phase would wreck the logistics of certainly one and possibly both of the Mediterranean projects.

Even with the hard facts of the situation in front of him, Mr. Churchill still tried to circumvent them, this time by an appeal to both the commander in chief of the Canadian forces in England, General McNaughton, and to the Canadian government. But they both agreed with the British Chiefs of Staff, and a few days later Sir Alan Brooke found his usually irrepressible master in the depths of despair.

What was the point of going on? Everybody blocked every avenue of progress toward victory and not one individual among his colleagues in the Cabinet, among his advisers from the army, the navy or the air force wanted to do anything at all! They could all always find excuses for doing nothing, but never accept reasons for swift action. Now with Russia at one end of the war machine and America at the other, it had all become too complicated, too cumbersome. He would just sit still from now on, and let the work come to him—which he did for nearly ten minutes, during which time the flow of tears streaming down his face dried up and light began to gleam again in his eyes as a new idea burgeoned in his mind.

What were Combined Operations doing in the light of the fiasco of the Dieppe Raid in August? Would not large-scale raids on the French coast serve both to restore morale among the commandos and perhaps draw German attention just a little bit away from the east?

"He is a wonderful mixture, and one never knows what mood he will be in next," wrote Sir Alan at the time. Much later he was to write, "I wonder if any historian of the future will ever be able to paint Winston in his true colours. It is a wonderful character, the most marvellous qualities and superhuman genius mixed with an astonishing lack of vision at times, and an impetuosity which, if not guided, must inevitably bring him into trouble again and again. . . . He is quite the most difficult man to work with that I have ever struck, but I would not have missed the chance of working with him for anything on earth."

Even so close to the dates of the attack at El Alamein and the Torch landings, there was still time for yet another complication to be introduced, another dire threat to be parried. During the previous April the island of Malta had been subjected to a concentrated bombing campaign in an effort to blunt the submarine and air attacks on Rommel's supply convoys, and at one time Axis plans had included those for Operation Herkules, a sea and airborne attack on the island intended to eliminate it once and for all from the Mediterranean battleground. However, the speed of Rommel's advance in June had persuaded Hitler that the operation would be unnecessary, but now, as more and more gasoline and arms sent from Italy to succor the Panzerarmee waiting for the onslaught at Alamein were sent to the bottom of the sea, he resolved to return to the attack.

For ten days from October 10, the skies above the island were rarely free of Luftwaffe fighters and bombers, and at the peak of the attack nearly five hundred sorties were flown against Malta in twelve hours. The RAF fighter defense squadrons fought with all the dedication of the Battle of Britain pilots two years before, but very soon it became obvious that unless more gasoline arrived soon, they would all be grounded. In this desperate situation the fastest naval minelayer at Gibraltar was loaded with as much fuel as she could carry and raced through "Bomb Alley," relying solely on her speed and luck to get her through. She arrived in the nick of time, though shortly afterward she was sunk going about her normal duties.

But even so, the plight of the island was still desperate. Lord Gort was now the governor of the island, and as he insisted on living on exactly the same rations as everyone else, despite his responsibilities and ever more onerous duties, he had lately lost so much weight that his once immaculate uniform hung on him like an ill-designed sack. His condition was shared by everyone there, civilian, fighter pilot, naval rating, or captain of the garrison. At the end of September it had been estimated that there was only food left for another month at the outside, and with the attention of the Luftwaffe so concentrated above Malta, there was not the slightest chance of getting supplies through from either end of the Mediterranean until the RAF had airstrips on the mainland within flying distance for their fighters to protect the convoys all the way.

And this would certainly not happen until after the Eighth Army had broken through the Axis lines opposite them and advanced some five hundred miles to at least as far as

Benghazi. As Field Marshal Smuts said in a message to Mr. Churchill at this time, "All depends on Alexander's success and on Torch being undertaken as soon as possible, consistent with firm prospect of success. We dare not fail with this venture on which so much depends for our victory."

Now the final moves were made for the two great enterprises. On October 21 the first convoy of supply ships left the American harbors en route for Casablanca, and four days later the long columns of merchant and naval ships carrying the men for the western task force under General Patton had assembled in the Bermuda area and begun the long trans-Atlantic passage that would take them into action. As they did so, other convoys steamed out of the Clyde and swung south around the north of Ireland, knowing that their next landfall would be the Straits of Gibraltar. Radio silence was total throughout.

But two days previously, the nighttime silence at Alamein had been shattered by a gigantic barrage from over a thousand guns as the long-awaited battle opened. It took the Axis forces opposite completely by surprise. Within hours their commander, General Stumme (for Rommel was in the hospital in Germany) was dead of a heart attack, and for twenty-four hours this was not realized. Only the superb efficiency of the Wehrmacht-trained Panzerarmee staff prevented a total collapse.

During that night, the Eighth Army infantry and engineers began the nerve-wracking job of punching two corridors through the defended mine fields at the northern end of the line, some of them five kilometers deep and all peppered with enemy machine-gun posts and under previously registered artillery fire. Montgomery's plan had called for both corridors to be completed by dawn for the armor to pass through, but, as he later admitted, perhaps he was asking too much of the infantry. The corridors were not clean through, so bitter fighting raged in the mine fields all the next day and the following night, by which time Rommel had returned to Egypt and resumed control of the Panzerarmee.

The detailed story of El Alamein has been told many times, but the main outlines of the battle remained quite close to those of Montgomery's revised forecast, which had not been given to Mr. Churchill. After three days of grueling battle, a deep bulge had been forced into the German defenses, and from this the Ninth Australian Division drove northward toward the coast, cutting off a large part of one of Rommel's crack divisions. The desperate attempts by the German forces to extricate their comrades led to three more days of what Montgomery called crumbling operations, battles of pure attrition where both sides were intent upon nothing less than the annihilation of the forces opposite. During this period, however, Montgomery withdrew one armored division and the New Zealanders to rest, and prepared them for Operation Supercharge, which would be a concentrated drive just south of the main battle area.

It was launched at 1:00 A.M. on November 2, and two days later the armor with the New Zealand Division in support was through the last defense along the Rahman Track and out into the open desert. Rommel's attempts to disengage had been thwarted by an order from the Führer that he was not to retreat one step, and which ended with the ruthless valediction: "As to your troops, you can show them no other road other than to victory or death."

For two more days the gallant successors of the original Afrika Korps struggled against the trap in which they were being crushed, but then Rommel's loyalty to them overrode his sense of obedience, and with his usual efficiency, he set in motion their withdrawal. By November 7, most of the German survivors were back south of Mersa Matruh, having commandeered all the available transport and left large numbers of Italian troops to their fate. Here they were saved by good fortune and bad weather.

They had been able to retire along the coast road, which gave them the advantage of a relatively hard surface for their trucks and other wheeled vehicles. To attempt to cut them off, British armored columns had to swing in from the south across soft sand in many places, and thus along longer routes at a slower pace. Moreover, it is part of the human condition that adrenalin flows faster in the veins of tired men escaping from a trap than in those of tired men closing it—as the South Africans had discovered when they escaped from the Gazala line the previous May; and now Rommel's men were helped by nature. Rain fell in torrents during the night of November 7, and by the morning the desert was a sodden bog. Thereafter, the Germans retired in well-conceived stages, always avoiding encirclement at the last moment, conscious that the implacable rule of movement in warfare was operating in their favor once more: supply lines shorten for retreating armies and lengthen to exactly the same extent for those pursuing them. But they never advanced again, and the only ones to see the Nile while the war lasted were those who had been taken prisoner.

For Mr. Churchill and the men at Whitehall, for Sir Alan Brooke especially, the last days of October 1942 stretched into eons of accumulating strain. In *The Turn of the Tide*, Sir Arthur Bryant's edited version of the *Alanbrooke War Diaries*, he quotes from Sir Alan's diary for the night of October 23.

> This evening after dinner, received call from War Office to say that Middle East attack had started. We are bound to have some desperately anxious moments. . . . There are great possibilities and great dangers. It may be the turning point of the War leading to further success combined with the North African attacks, or it may mean nothing. If it fails I don't quite know how I shall bear it. I have pinned such hopes on these two offensives.

"I remember that evening," he wrote afterward, "as if it were yesterday, and can see myself sitting at my writing table in my Westminster Gardens flat, finishing those last lines and remaining seated staring into space."

For Mr. Churchill the strain of leading his country for two and a half years of perhaps the greatest danger she had ever faced now reached its climax. If the attack at El Alamein or the impending landings in North Africa should fail, then so would his own career. He would be toppled from power, and the power would then pass to others who he felt sure would prove in the end to be lesser mortals than himself. Not only would his own life be reduced to waste and ashes, but the hardship and perils that his beloved country had faced since 1940 would now be extended far into the future. The weight of the world sat on the prime minister's shoulders during that first week of El Alamein, and on October 29 it seemed likely to crush him, for he still believed that Montgomery's plan scheduled a breakout ten days after the commencement of

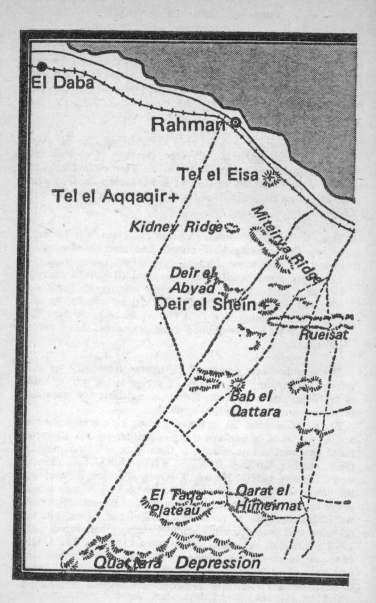

MEDITERRANEAN
SEA

El Alamein

Burg el Arab

Ridge

Alam el Halfa Ridge

N
W   E
S

EL ALAMEIN
MILES

0   10   20   30

the battle (Montgomery had rescheduled it for twelve days) and now the latest news from the front was that he was *withdrawing whole divisions*!

The storm burst over Sir Alan Brooke's head early that morning. What was his protégé Montgomery doing, allowing the battle to peter out? Why was he taking troops out of the battle? Why did he say he would break out in seven days if he only intended to fight in a halfhearted manner?

"Haven't we got a single general who can win even one battle?" Churchill cried, and for a moment Sir Alan thought he was going to hit him.

The storm passed quickly then, but at the Chiefs of Staff meeting that afternoon it blew up again, and it needed the cool, even cold, common sense of the great South African leader, Field Marshal Smuts, who had flown up to Cairo and then accompanied them all back to London, to calm the atmosphere. When turned to for his comments at the end of Brooke's defense of Montgomery's conduct of the battle so far, he remarked, "I am in entire agreement with all the opinions the C.I.G.S. has expressed." Mr. Churchill relaxed and accepted his viewpoint.

From then on, the news from the front improved as every hour passed until the moment came when a cable from Alexander informed the prime minister that the enemy's front was broken and that those enemy forces not captured were in full retreat. The heartfelt message of congratulation sent in reply contained the following passage:

If the reasonable hopes of your telegram are maintained, and wholesale captures of the enemy and a general retreat are apparent, I propose to ring the bells all over Britain for the first time this war. Try to give me the moment to do this in the next few days. At least 20,000 prisoners would be necessary.

Two days later came the longed-for message:

General Alexander to Prime Minister   6 Nov 42

Ring out the bells! Prisoners estimated now 20,000, tanks 350, guns 400, M.T. several thousand. Our advanced mobile forces are south of Mersa Matruh. Eighth Army is advancing.

In fact, Mr. Churchill decided to wait. Operation Torch was about to hit the North African beaches. He would wait until success was registered there.

He did not have too long to wait. Incredibly, the western task force crossed the entire Atlantic without discovery or attack, the convoys from the Clyde linked up exactly on schedule, began steaming through the Straits of Gibraltar on November 5, and with the exception of one transport, which was torpedoed 150 miles from Algiers (but not sunk, and its assault force of 800 American infantry was immediately taken aboard a landing craft to play their part in the attack), every ship was in place off its landing point on time.

Reception was mixed and the reverse of what had been expected, for the Americans at Casablanca and at Oran were resisted by the French, while the combined British and American force at Algiers landed with hardly a shot being fired and were quickly in control of their beaches. What French resistance there was was patchy everywhere, and although occasionally fierce, it never lasted long, due to basic uncertainty among the French commanders, many of whom wished to cooperate with the Allies in order to rid themselves of the Axis, but all of whom wished to act within the framework of French military law and obey orders from properly constituted authority.

That authority could only stem from Marshall Pétain, but by a piece of astonishingly good fortune for the Allies, his deputy, Admiral Darlan, was in Algiers visiting his son, who had recently contracted poliomyelitis. The admiral's immediate reaction was not promising: "I have known for a long time that the British were stupid, but I always believed the Americans were more intelligent!" His reputation as a collaborator with the Nazis would have made him a most unwelcome ally had he not been so important, but by a combination of diplomacy and plain straightforward bullying, Mark Clark persuaded him that his best course of action would be cooperation, and at 11:20 on the morning of November 10 he ordered an end to all French resistance in North Africa.

Generally he was obeyed in Morocco and Algeria, although the extraordinary rapidity of the German reaction in Tunis held up matters there, but the whole picture clarified when the news came in that Hitler's infuriated reaction to

Torch was to order German troops to move into the unoccupied zone of southern France, which they did on November 11. This, in the opinion of the French Command in North Africa, relieved them of their pledge of obedience to Marshall Pétain who they judged, quite rightly, would from then on be acting under duress; from then on the Allied opening moves went smoothly. By November 12 British airborne forces had taken the airfield at Bône, and five days later were at Souk el Arba three hundred miles east of Algiers, while the 503rd U.S. Parachute Regiment had dropped at Youks les Bains nearly a hundred miles to the south and within two days had taken Gafsa airfield inside Tunisia.

Behind them, the American troops were shaking out and moving up, and the British First Army was commandeering every piece of transport it could find to lift supporting units forward to help the airborne formations. There would obviously be some tough fighting ahead as the Luftwaffe was already making things difficult, and German and Italian troops were pouring into Tunisia, but the landings had been accomplished, the indigenous natives were certainly not hostile, the French were cooperating and showing themselves more than willing to fight the Germans if they could be given modern weapons, and the Eighth Army was hot in pursuit of the Afrika Korps.

Perhaps the First and Eighth Armies would meet somewhere in Libya by Christmas?

To Mr. Churchill and the Chiefs of Staff, the success of the sea crossings alone had seemed a miracle, and if the first news of French resistance was a sobering factor for a few hours, the announcement that Darlan was present and apparently prepared to cooperate sent hopes rising to an unprecedented height. He was known to have been violently anti-British all his life and since 1940 had been vilified throughout the Allied press and propaganda systems as an arch-collaborator with the Nazis, but as Churchill had said to Mark Clark in London, "If I could meet Darlan, much as I hate him, I would cheerfully crawl on my hands and knees for a mile if by doing so I could get him to bring that fleet of his into the circle of the Allied forces."

President Roosevelt's reaction to the Anglo-American acceptance of Darlan's help was the same, and when public reaction in America questioned the decision, he quoted an old proverb of the Orthodox Church.

"My children, it is permitted you in time of grave danger to walk with the devil until you have crossed the bridge."

By November 15, 1942, Mr. Churchill had decided that the bridge, if not crossed, was safe. That night, for the first time since 1940, the church bells rang out across England to celebrate what he was later to call "the turning of the Hinge of Fate."

CHAPTER NINE

A carping historical critic might, with the benefit of hindsight, declare Mr. Churchill's bell-ringing order both ill-timed and unjustified. Certainly it served to lift the spirits of the British people after a time of considerable despondency, but on the other hand it hardly signaled in a period of halcyon success, for Allied inexperience quickly proved no match for German speed of reaction and professionalism.

Within two days of the Torch landings, German troops were occupying commanding positions along the perimeter of a bridgehead effectively guarding Bizerta and Tunis, and other forces were flooding ashore in the south to protect Sfax and Gabès. By the time the main Allied forces had arrived to support the gallant but frail airborne thrusts, German battalions were solidly in position, soon to be immeasurably helped by torrential winter rains, which effectively swept away all chances of that quick and easy linkup between the First Army and the Eighth, the latter in Benghazi by November 20, but still a long way from Tripoli. There was after all no chance of that linkup by Christmas, and soon it became obvious that there was little hope of one for many months.

Neither had Mr. Churchill's fondest hope been realized. The French fleet did not sail out from Toulon to join the Allied navies, for Admiral de Labord was far too loyal to Marshall Pétain to move without his direct order, and in the absence of such an order he ignored a suggestion cabled to him by Darlan that he sail with the fleet to Oran. On the other hand, despite his anti-British sentiments, he had no intention of allowing his command to fall into Hitler's hands. When German forces moved in to the unoccupied zone, he gave orders for scuttling charges to be brought to readiness in every ship under his command, and when on November 27 elements of three panzer divisions swept down on the Toulon naval establishments, the order "Scuttle! Scuttle! Scuttle!"

was flashed from the masthead of practically every ship in the dockyard. Seventy-three ships including one battleship, two battle cruisers, seven cruisers, twenty-nine destroyers, and sixteen submarines went to the bottom of the harbor, where they remained until the war was practically over. But they did not fight on the Allied side.

And if the bell ringing really did celebrate the "turning of the Hinge of Fate," that development in itself betokened something of great significance for the British people in general and for Mr. Churchill in particular.

For three years Britain had fought the European conflict virtually alone. Although since Barbarossa she had had one ally and since Pearl Harbor two, in a narrow and immediate sense both allies had up to that moment been rather more of a hindrance than a help. A great deal of war material badly needed by the British forces had gone instead to Russia, whose reparative cooperation could hardly have been called close, and despite American generosity, it had not been until almost the end of 1942 that U.S. armies came into action against the main enemy. Thus, Britain had been the core of western opposition to the Axis since 1939, and Mr. Churchill her leader and inspiration throughout many months of danger and near defeat.

Now with the first intimations of victory, however long delayed, the balance began to change significantly.

Except under very special circumstances, battles—let alone wars—are won only by big battalions, and the German Wehrmacht of the Second World War could in the final analysis only be beaten by the combination of Russian manpower and American industrial might. Britain had held the ring—and it could be argued that she had done so for only just long enough; had the strain gone on for much longer she might have broken. But now that the tide was turning, and her role in the conflict would inevitably be reduced in comparison with that of the two giants who had joined her. And so would be her leader's standing and influence in the world.

That these facts were recognized at the top level is demonstrated by the agreement, strongly backed by Mr. Churchill, that despite the fact that when eventually the First and Eighth Armies joined hands there would be only six American divisions in North Africa as against twelve British and Commonwealth (though two more American divisions would join before the end of the campaign), the combined force would be commanded by an American, Lieutenant General Eisenhower. Although he had never commanded a formation in battle himself, he would have as subordinates both Alexander and Montgomery, plus a whole host of more junior generals, all battle-hardened in two world wars.

Yet no one seriously questioned the decision (Montgomery had a few cryptic comments to make), for it was a gesture toward the future, toward the not too distant time when four gigantic American armies would move up to the Rhine between Strasbourg and München Gladbach, while the only British army in the field—in conjunction with the Canadian army—was holding the sixty miles from there up to Nijmegen.

Another recognition of the realities to come had been made in a cable from Mr. Churchill to President Roosevelt while the planning for Torch was still in progress.

Former Naval Person to   15 Sept 42
President Roosevelt

I entirely agree with your political outlook on "Torch." It is sound unless we are forestalled. There is no sign that the enemy is aware, and the mood of France is now at its very best. I count the days. In the whole of "Torch", military and political, I consider myself your lieutenant, asking only to put my view-point plainly before you. ... We British will come in only as and when you judge expedient. This is an American enterprise in which we are your helpmeets.

It was a relationship that was to extend in both time and space well beyond the boundaries of Torch.

Toward the end of November, President Roosevelt suggested that the time was approaching for a three-power conference at the top level in order to agree on strategy for the further prosecution of the war. According to Harry Hopkins he also felt that it was time he took advantage of the opportunity for travel and few days rest; whether the American public liked it or not, the conference would be held outside the United States. Both Iceland and Khartoum were suggested, but in the end a far more convenient location was chosen—a well-guarded and spacious luxury hotel just outside Casablanca.

M. Stalin, however, had decided that he could not leave Russia at that particular moment, so only the leaders of the Western Allies would be present—though both were well aware of the suspicions that would be generated in Moscow should they fail to keep the Russians fully informed of their discussions.

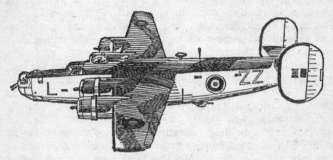

Liberator

Mr. Churchill and his closest advisers left England on January 12 in a Libertor that had not been adapted for the journey and was thus rather uncomfortable, but despite a crisis when a heater threatened not only to burn the prime minister's toes but also to set fire to the blankets—and probably blow the plane apart by igniting the gasoline fumes—they arrived quite safely the following morning.

The president arrived on the afternoon of January 14, the following day General Eisenhower flew in after a rather hazardous flight from Algiers, and two days later General Alexander arrived with excellent news from the Eighth Army front and what Mr. Churchill described as his "easy, smiling grace," which won everybody's confidence.

This was probably as well, for it quickly became obvious that there were serious differences of opinion between the American and British Chiefs of Staff, which it was going to take a great deal of argument and discussion to resolve. There were also differences in attitude, which proved then and for a long time afterward extremely troublesome, caused by the possibly unconscious feeling among the Americans that as they would soon be putting the larger armies into the field, they also assumed the better part of military wisdom.

Britain's historical experience of world strategy and her recent experience in battle were never denied in open speech or discussion, but it would seem that between the top American leaders they were both suspected and ignored in private conversations and were probably absent from the minds of their planners. The result would have been a resounding defeat for the British point of view had it not been for the debating skills of Sir Alan Brooke and the fact that there were several differences of opinion among the Americans themselves.

Admiral King, for instance, was still convinced that the correct strategy for his own country was to defeat the Japanese first and leave Europe to its own devices until the East was secure. And despite the unqualified decision to the contrary by the president and the order by the Combined Chiefs of Staff that only a holding operation should be mounted in the Pacific, he continued to divert the bulk of newly constructed American shipping, especially the vital landing craft, away from the European theater.

General Marshall, on the other hand, was fully committed to the concept Europe First, but although he had agreed to abandon Sledgehammer in the face of the July disasters in the desert, and had not opposed Torch, he regarded any further operations in the Mediterranean as a wasteful dissipation of effort. In his mind only a cross-Channel invasion of France with twenty or thirty divisions would win the war, and to further this he had done everything he could to expedite Operation Bolero (the buildup of American forces in Britain and Ulster) and felt strongly that Operation Roundup, as the proposed invasion was then called, should take place in 1943.

In this, as late as the previous month, he had had the full support of Mr. Churchill, whose basic stance then and throughout the entire war was that as many Allied troops as possible should be in action against the Nazis, all the time. However, before the meetings at Casablanca, the combined British Chiefs of Staff had persuaded him that the American armies in Britain—who would undoubtedly have to bear the main burden of the fighting on the Continent—would be neither numerous nor well-trained enough until the spring of 1944 at the earliest and that any attempt before then would result in a calamitous failure.

But as Mr. Churchill had once attempted to cable Auchinleck in one of his moments of more extreme frustration, "Armies are not meant to stand about doing nothing." Especially Anglo-American armies when their Russian allies were holding the enemy at Stalingrad in a titanic conflict that held the attention of the world and compelled the admiration of everyone outside Germany. So where would the First and Eighth Armies fight after the destruction of the German-Italian armies in North Africa?

It was here that the strategic convictions and unyielding arguments of Sir Alan Brooke took command. At no time did he believe that Germany would be defeated without that major invasion of the Continent followed by a drive straight at the heart of the Nazi empire so firmly advocated by General Marshall and his compatriots. But there was a great deal to be done to adjust the balance between Allied and Axis forces before even the landing operations in France held any chance of success.

Not only must the buildup of American forces in Britain be continued for some time and its rate accelerated (and where was the shipping to come from with so high a proportion going to the Pacific?), but both they and the British armies at home needed far more training, more and newer equipment, and time to master its capabilities. But even more important were the measures to be taken now to weaken Germany, both by bombing her industrial centers (and at the end of 1942 American planes had never been over Germany in strength and the RAF Bomber Force numbered only some 800 first-line planes) and by forcing her to dissipate her strength.

Already twenty-six Axis divisions were permanently stationed in the Balkans to hold down the turbulent Greeks, Albanians, and above all the Yugoslav Partisans under Marshal Tito. The Greek islands were jointly controlled by German and Italian garrisons, but British raiding forces had already discovered that the Italians were disaffected and more than willing to surrender when attacked. And there was every good reason to believe that in Italy itself what enthusiasm there had ever been for the war had almost evaporated.

Therefore, in Sir Alan's opinion the correct strategy once North Africa had been cleared of Axis troops would be the invasion of either Sicily or Sardinia (he preferred Sicily himself), followed probably by the invasion of the Italian mainland or whatever other step seemed most likely to knock Italy out of the war. This would serve to attract German divisions at least to the Brenner Pass and the Italian border with Austria—if not down into Italy itself—thus weakening Nazi strength in France and on the Russian front; it would open the entire Mediterranean passage to allied shipping, it would threaten southern Europe from the Pyrenees to the Balkans, and it might even induce Turkey to throw in her lot with the Allies and thus make her landing grounds available, from which Allied bombers could eventually strike at the Ploesti oil fields and the Danube basin.

And to support Sir Alan at Casablanca were not only his colleagues on the Chiefs of Staff Committee with whom he had gone over the arguments time and time again, but a large planning and cipher staff who had traveled from Britain in a specially adapted 6,000-ton Headquarters and Communications ship, and who were available to produce accurate figures and extrapolations upon any aspect of the situation that might arise in the course of the discussions.

The Casablanca Conference lasted until January 23—nine days of close discussion and hard work for everyone, interspersed with pleasant talks over excellent meals or on relaxed walks around the port or to the nearby beaches. The most concentrated work was done by the Chiefs of Staff and their immediate advisers, but every evening president and prime minister held meetings at which the day's conclusions were presented and further discussed, and often the following day one or the other of them would use his influence to smooth over the main differences.

The results were remarkable—far better than many had thought likely before the conference began, infinitely better than had seemed possible at some of the more difficult phases of the conferences itself.

was granted. The party set off on the first stage of the journey at 6:30 P.M. that evening, Mr. Churchill's bouyant mood continuing and finding expression in a cable he sent to Mr. Attlee and Mr. Eden reading: "We are just over the Atlas Mountains, which are gleaming with their sunlit snows. You can imagine how much I wish I were going to be with you tomorrow on the bench. But duty calls!"

They arrived the following morning at Cairo and went to breakfast at the embassy where Mrs. Lampson, the ambassador's wife, offered the prime minister a cup of tea. This would not do, however, for as he explained, he had since dawn already smoked two cigars and drunk two large whiskey and sodas, so what he would really prefer would be some dry white wine—of which he promptly drained a glassful as though it were water. Presumably after almost sixty years of such treatment, his liver had got used to it.

The meeting with the Turks was pleasant, agreeable, and totally unproductive. The Turkish leaders were well aware of the benefits of neutrality, of the enormous power that victory would give to the Soviet Union (for whose intentions they had exactly the same suspicions as their predecessors had had for the czars), and of the still tenuous protection the Western Allies could give them if they provoked the anger of Nazi Germany. But their protestations of goodwill were profuse and sincere, and nothing could disturb Mr. Churchill's euphoria. He returned to Cairo via Cyprus, arriving on February 1, and had little difficulty in persuading Brooke that as the Eighth Army had at last entered Tripoli on January 23, they should both call there on the way home to congratulate Montgomery and see how his victorious army was feeling.

They found them all in high fettle. Montgomery was bouncing with confidence and more than willing to expound not only on his own plans for driving the Eighth Army forward into Tunisia, but also his convictions as to the best way for Eisenhower and his subordinate generals to play their parts in the final annihilation of the Axis forces in Africa. As for the army, Mr. Churchill and Sir Alan, accompanied by both Montgomery and Alexander, inspected first the Fifty-first Highland Division and later Bernard Freyberg's New Zealanders, and the difference in every aspect of their appearance between the time when last the two men had seen them before Alam Halfa and now was remarkable. Of the Highlanders, Brooke later wrote:

Then they were still pink and white; now they are bronzed warriors of many battles and of a victorious advance. I have seldom seen a finer body of men or one that looked prouder of being soldiers. . . . The whole division was most beautifully turned out, and might have been in barracks for the last three months instead of having marched some 1,200 miles.

They then went on to call at Algiers—somewhat to Eisenhower's apprehension as Security had warned them that there were strong rumors of a plot to assassinate Mr. Churchill while he was there. After talks with the new French leaders and with Admiral Cunningham, who had now been appointed to command all naval forces in the Mediterranean, Mr. Churchill and Sir Alan left in two separate planes for England. They landed at Lyneham on the morning of February 7.

Five days later Mr. Churchill complained of a headache and a sore throat, three days later he was obviously ill but still insisting upon presiding over a Cabinet meeting, but by February 16 it was quite obvious to both Sir Charles Wilson and the specialist he had called in that the prime minister had pneumonia. Despite the attempts of both the British and American press to dub him the world's worst patient, he obeyed all instructions as long as he was given an adequate explanation for their necessity and was quite amused when the specialist breezily announced that he always referred to pneumonia as "the old man's friend."

"Pray explain," demanded his patient.

"Oh, because it takes them off so quickly," came the reply—which apparently established the speaker high in Mr. Churchill's favor.

But the strain under which everybody had been laboring during the last months was exacting its tolls. Both President Roosevelt and Sir Alan Brooke had to take to their beds at the end of February, and it was a few days into March before all three of them were back in their offices—to find that matters were not yet progressing as well as they had hoped. U-boat action was still taking a dreadful toll in the Atlantic: shipping losses in February had reached 413,062 tons and in

March were to rise to nearly 700,000 tons. And there was little sign of the longed-for linkup in Tunis, let alone the capitulation of the Axis forces there.

Logistics were still posing enormous problems. The Eighth Army was now 200 miles past Tripoli, but their main supply base was still the Delta, and the distance from Tripoli to Cairo was the same as that from Whitehall to the Kremlin. Benghazi was in full use as a port by now, but until Tripoli was in similar shape, supplies for the forward divisions had to travel along a single road stretching the distance from London to Vienna—and every hoped-for advance would lengthen that road. Already, Montgomery had been forced to strip all transport from the reserve corps in order to keep the forward corps sufficiently mobile to rebuff Rommel should the latter suddenly attack, and it had been with some relief that the Eighth Army heard of his lightning attack on the American First Armored Division at Kasserine Pass in Tunisia.

It proved a bitter introduction to battle for the G.I.s, who were roughly flung back some thirty miles, losing half their tanks and guns in the process, but within days the ground was recovered by joint British and American action, and from then on, slowly but with ever-growing certainty, the ring around the Axis forces in Tunisia was to tighten. On March 20 the Eighth Army attack on the Mareth line opened, eight days later the First Army reopened the offensive that had been stopped by the winter weather three months before, and on April 8, patrols from the U.S. II Corps, probing south from Gafsa, met troops of the Twelfth Lancers from the Eighth Army's First Armored Division. The linkup had at last taken place. And Rommel, a sick and exhausted man, had now left North Africa for good, his place in command of the Axis forces taken by General von Arnim.

Rommel's removal from the scene of his greatest triumphs might be seen as a token for the future, for from that time on, the entire war situation improved for the Allies.

The most immediate, spectacular, and indeed significant change took place at sea. Four months before, Britain's most famous submarine officer, Admiral Sir Max Horton, had been appointed commander in chief of Western Approaches, the most crucial post in the anti-U-boat war. By the ruthless stripping of every naval command and rigorous selection of officers and men, he assembled six support or hunter-killer

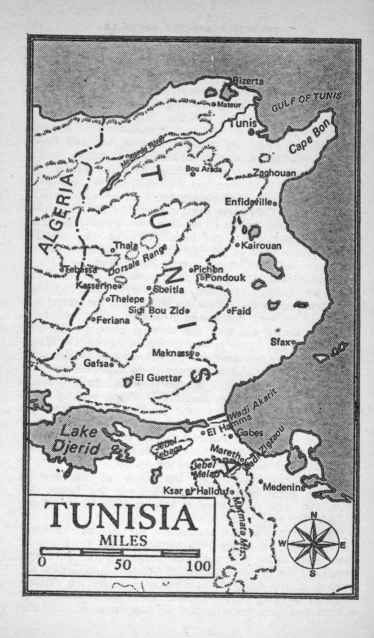

groups of destroyers, and during the winter had trained them into close cooperation teams with one object—the hunting and destruction of U-boats.

Aided by the latest centimetric radar devices now at last coming in worthwhile numbers from the factories, these teams concentrated in April in the "black pit" in the middle of the Atlantic, where air cover was still almost impossible, and began their attack on the German wolf packs. They were immediately successful, and that month the shipping losses were halved, while in May they dropped to below 300,000 tons. At the end of that month, Admiral Doenitz withdrew his U-boat force from such dangerous waters, for they had lost forty of their number in two months. So dramatic was the shift in fortune that in June, Allied shipping losses in the Atlantic were one-twentieth of those in March.

And as the hunter-killer groups had opened their attack,* so the drives by the First and Eighth Armies in North Africa gathered strength and speed. By the end of that month the thousands of German troops whom Hitler had thrown into the battle there were penned into a narrowing bridgehead around Bizerta, Tunis, and the Cape Bon Peninsula. The battles for Enfidaville and Longstop Hill had been fought, and behind the besieged Panzerarmee, the Royal Navy was gathering for Operation Retribution, a Dunkirk in reverse for which Admiral Cunningham had already issued the categoric instructions: "Sink, burn, destroy! Let nothing pass!"

On the left the U.S. II Corps, now commanded by Lt. Gen. Omar Bradley (Patton had been relieved to plan for the invasion of Sicily), was poised to drive along the coast and up through Mateur toward Bizerta. First Army held the center of the line and the onus of prime attack through the Medjerda Gap toward Tunis, while the Eighth Army held the southern sector reaching the coast at Enfidaville, its task to hold the attention of von Arnim away from the more vital areas, to which had been sent the most famous of the Eighth Army formations—7th Armored Division, 4th Indian Division and 201st Guards Brigade—on loan to the First Army in a generous gesture by Montgomery, anxious as always to help his

*For a full account of these hunter killer groups read ESCORT COMMANDER by Terence Robertson who tells the story of Walker R.N. He was the man who beat the U-Boats down. Another volume in The Bantam War Book Series.

friend and commander, Alexander, in the last battle on African soil.

The onslaught began at 3:00 A.M. on the morning of May 6 with a concentrated artillery bombardment in the center under which two brigades of the Fourth Indian Division crept forward toward the known positions of a regiment of Panzer Grenadiers. They were on them within an hour, the leading companies of Gurkhas cutting their way through the outposts and into the main enemy positions with their kukris, Bren-carriers bringing up the support companies and then fanning out to find the limits of the position. As they did so, they made contact with the British division on their right flank,

Bren Gun Carrier

moving forward parallel with them, and then each division advanced on each side of the central valley. By 9:30 A.M. they were through the main enemy defenses, and the tanks of Seventh Armored Division could pass through and drive for Tunis.

For von Arnim and his troops, it was quickly obvious that the end had come. Their thirteen sadly depleted divisions were being attacked by nineteen divisions at full strength; they had only 130 panzers left and were being attacked by over 1,200 Allied tanks; 500 guns defended them against 1,500; and only 500 planes were available to hold back air assaults mounted by over 3,000. Yet they fought at first with all the efficiency and valor that had distinguished the Afrika Korps from the beginning, the only evidence of their decline the ever-weakening counterattacks when they had been pushed off a hill or driven out of a valley.

But within two days both Bizerta and Tunis had been captured. Tunis was first entered by reconnaissance patrols of the Eleventh Hussars, the squadrons that had opened the desert war against the Italians almost exactly three years before. Their final drive had taken place so quickly that they surprised German soldiers walking through the streets arm in arm with their girlfriends.

To the north the Americans were mopping up in Bizerta itself and clearing out the last Axis posts in the hills and lakes close to Mateur, while to the south the Eighth Armored Division and the Guards Brigade were racing for the Cape Bon Peninsula where for a few days the last remnants of Panzerarmee Afrika held out. Then on May 12, von Arnim was captured by a unit from the Fourth Indian Division. The commander of the famous Ninetieth Light Division, Major General Graf von Sponek, was taken by his old enemies the New Zealanders. The following day the titular head of the Axis forces in North Africa, the Italian Field Marshal Giovanni Messe also surrendered to the famous New Zealander, Lt. Gen. Bernard Freyberg.

It was claimed at the time that 250,000 German and Italian soldiers gave themselves up to the Anglo-American armies in North Africa, only a few attempting to escape to Sicily and of those, seventy-seven were scooped out of the sea by the Royal Navy and over a hundred later found marooned on one of the offshore islands. Those who surrendered in the north to the Americans or the First Army were subjected to a certain amount of ridicule and mockery by the comparative newcomers to the war, but those in the south—especially the Germans of the Ninetieth Light or the Fifteenth or Twenty-first Panzer Divisions, who had been among the first of Rommel's troops—were watched in sympathetic silence by the men of the Eighth Army who had fought them across nearly two thousand miles of hills and deserts and shared too many experiences with them to feel hatred or indeed much triumph.

That evening General Alexander sent a cable to the prime minister reading:

Sir:

It is my duty to report that the Tunisian campaign is over. All enemy resistance has ceased. We are masters of the North African shores.

The Desert War, the last successful land campaign in the west in which the British army was to play the senior role, was over.

CHAPTER TEN

Mr. Churchill was not in London to receive General Alexander's momentous cable, for the onrush of events had made it obvious that another meeting of the heads of government was essential. At Casablanca no agreement had been made as to the deployment of the armies after Sicily had been conquered, and as plans for Operation Husky, as this next phase of the Mediterranean war was called, had now reached an advanced stage, the time had come for a firm decision. Sir Charles Wilson had protested at the idea of Mr. Churchill flying to Washington so soon after his illness, so a portion of the upper decks of the *Queen Mary* was sealed off (the other passengers were German prisoners of war en route for Canada), and the entire party, which included Sir Alan Brooke and the other Chiefs of Staff plus the usual complement of advisers and cipher and communication staff, boarded the ship on May 5.

As usual, the voyage was fully occupied with planning conferences, and from reports sent them by Sir John Dill, it was quite obvious that a long series of arguments was inevitable. Many of the decisions made at Casablanca had either become the subject of dissent back in Washington or were being interpreted by Admiral King and his naval colleagues in a manner not intended.

In this Admiral King was being encouraged by the chairman of the American Chiefs of Staff, Admiral Leahy, who had been prevented by illness from attending the Casablanca Conference and would seem to have considered himself therefore absolved from following those of its conclusions with which he disagreed. He in turn received more support from the American secretary of war, Mr. Stimson, a dogmatic seventy-six-year-old, who despite frequent protestations to the contrary, would appear to have been one of those Americans who believed all Europeans and especially Britons to be

161

devious in character, cunning in thought, and totally ruthless in exploitation of the simple, upright, and fundamentally straightforward and honest Americans.

He also possessed to a strong degree the old man's ability to hear only what he was certain he was going to hear. One report of a conversation he had with Mr. Churchill about the proposed cross-Channel invasion of France (to which he insisted upon referring as Operation Roundhammer) claimed that Mr. Churchill "was obsessed with the idea of proving to history that invasion of the Continent by way of the Balkans was wise strategy and would repair whatever damage history now records for Churchill's misfortune at the Dardanelles in the last War." Stimson also used his position to question closely the British planners for Roundup. When they agreed that there were undoubted difficulties and dangers about the operation, he promptly claimed that such agreement was proof of the British intention to avoid all commitment to an invasion of France, a claim that he also buttressed by announcing that Churchill had frequently confessed to him that one of his recurrent nightmares was of the English Channel full of the floating corpses of defeated allies!

In view of the prime minister's past harrying of his generals to fling their armies into battle as quickly as possible; of his support for American demands for Sledgehammer in 1942 and Roundup in 1943 until his Chiefs of Staff had persuaded him of their fundamental impracticability; and of the pressures he would soon be applying to them to put their armies ashore at the earliest possible moment on Sicily, on the toe of Italy, at Salerno, and anywhere else he could suggest, Mr. Stimson's fixations would have been laughable had they not been held at so influential a level. As it was, his constant reiteration of his conviction that the British would do everything they could to avoid an invasion of France and direct all possible effort toward the eastern Mediterranean did unnecessary harm to Anglo-American relations.

It also tended at times to reduce argument and debate to almost farcical levels. It had been agreed at Casablanca that some 80,000 American troops would be sent to England during the spring, but largely as a result of Admiral King's diversion of so much American shipping to the Pacific, only 15,000 had arrived. During the opening days of this Second Washington Conference (to be known as Trident), charges by one or two of the more vociferous American champions of

Roundup that Britain was not fully behind the operation were countered by the flat statement that unless American troops arrived at the agreed rate, then Roundup would be impossible anyway; to be answered in its turn by the claim that there was no point in sending G.I.s to Britain if Britain did not intend to put them across the Channel!

Fortunately, neither General Marshall nor President Roosevelt would countenance such elliptical thought, although at one point the former did state quite categorically that if Britain's strategy was really to "waste time in the Mediterranean," the American forces might well be better employed in the Pacific. Such indeed was the atmosphere of tension during the opening days of Trident that Brooke was quite relieved when discussions left the realm of Mediterranean strategy to concentrate on matters further east in Burma, and especially in China, a country in whose military potential many of the Americans had an almost mystical belief.

Even so, a week after the opening session, the difficulties of arriving at a series of conclusions to put to president and prime minister with the support of all appeared insuperable, until General Marshall realized that one of the main blocks to agreement was the number of people present at the meetings. The American Chiefs of Staff had appreciated the value of the large staff with which the British had been attended at Casablanca, and for Trident they produced their own legions, many of whom sat behind their principals at the meeting, exercising a silent pressure upon them all the time. On May 19 he proposed that the afternoon session should be off the record and for the Chiefs of Staff only. By the evening acceptable conclusions had been arrived at.

These reiterated the overall aim of bringing about as quickly as possible the unconditional surrender of the Axis powers in Europe, and although Admiral King still obtained a statement of aims for the Pacific, which he thought would give him the necessary leeway to continue his own chosen path, this section contained a rider to the effect that any considerable extension of the existing pressure against the Japanese would require the permission of the Combined Chiefs of Staff. Perhaps he felt that interpretation of the word considerable would be left to him, and in any case he exacted a price from the British; they agreed to mount sea-borne assaults on Ramree Island and Akyab on the coast of Burma.

As far as operations against Italy were concerned, however, all that the British could achieve was the resolution:

. . . that the Allied Commander-in-Chief, North Africa should be instructed to mount such operations in exploitation of 'Husky' as are best calculated to eliminate Italy from the war and to contain the maximum number of German forces. Each specific operation will be subject to the approval of the Combined Chiefs of Staff. The Allied Commander-in-Chief in North Africa may use for his operations all those forces available in the Mediterranean area except for four American and three British divisions which will be held in readiness from the 1st November onwards for withdrawal to take part in operations from the United Kingdom.

Moreover, it was stated that the three American heavy bomber groups would be returned to England as soon as Husky was over whatever the developing situation and that if "such operations in exploitation" required much in the way of shipping, then this would have to be the subject of special permission from the Combined Chiefs of Staff, to be applied for in advance.

The only aspect of affairs that favored the British point of view at this moment was that General Marshall had planned to visit the Southwest Pacific theater as soon as Trident was over, and upon the president's suggestion he agreed to travel with the prime minister to Algiers en route—for with the eventual arrival of Alexander's cable, Mr. Churchill announced that he and his party must go there as soon as possible, both to congratulate all concerned and to expedite if necessary the invasion of Sicily.

"I have no more pleasant memories of the war than the eight days spent in Algiers and Tunis," Mr. Churchill was later to write, and if a great deal of the enjoyment was due to the air of victory in which the party moved, a portion was undoubtedly the result of the main British success there.

However strongly General Marshall might feel that the Mediterranean theater should be closed down once Sicily had been occupied, he was not proof against the facts of the hour. The British had three times as many troops in the area as the Americans, four times as many warships, and an equal air strength, yet at no time was General Eisenhower's position as supreme commander questioned, and full attention was paid to his views at all meetings, perhaps, it must be admitted, because they accorded strongly with Sir Alan Brooke's.

The Sicily landings were due to take place in early July, and Eisenhower felt sure that the whole island would be in Allied hands by mid-August. What were the divisions to do then? Even when the seven divisions of the Mediterranean armies had returned to England as agreed at Trident, at least twelve fully experienced fighting divisions would remain in the area. Now four French divisions were being reequipped, and two Polish divisions in Persia were ready and eager for action.

Were they, and indeed all the Anglo-American forces in Europe, to do nothing until Operation Roundup, now obviously unlikely to take place until the late spring of 1944? With the Russian armies still fighting gigantic battles on the eastern front?

There was little General Marshall could do but signify agreement—guarded certainly, in view of the strong feelings back in Washington—and he could not give formal permission then and there for an attack across the Straits of Messina to the toe of Italy as soon as Sicily was occupied. Instead, he suggested that plans should be drawn up for such a crossing and also for the invasion of Sardinia—and a decision made in the light of the German defense of Sicily and the progress of the Allied armies there, nearer to the date, when either or both should take place. But at least he agreed that in order for military pressure to be kept on Italy to force her out of the war, the Mediterranean theater should not be closed down.

With this both Mr. Churchill and Sir Alan Brooke were for the moment content, and an atmosphere of warm friendliness developed, only slightly threatened by the return of Montgomery from leave in England on June 3. One way and another, the Eighth Army commander had been making himself thoroughly unpopular at all levels of the American staff, both by his outspoken criticisms of what he regarded as their lack of professionalism, and by his quite astonishing insensitivity.

It had started with his reaction to Eisenhower's original plans for Operation Husky. It must be said that these reflected in some degree the lack of experience in battle of those who drew them up, but Montgomery's dismissal of them as "a dog's breakfast which broke every commonsense rule of practical fighting," was tactless, especially as it achieved considerable publicity.

But the gaffe to which the Americans in general and Eisenhower in particular took most exception was the affair of the Flying Fortress.

B-17 Flying Fortress

At some time during the previous March, Eisenhower's chief of staff, Major General Walter Bedell Smith had announced at a planning conference that if the Eighth Army cleared Sousse by April 12, the date Montgomery had forecast, Montgomery would deserve a Flying Fortress as a prize. Montgomery's forecast, as so often, proved accurate, and he immediately cabled Bedell Smith to the effect that he would appreciate immediate delivery, a request that was at first laughed off.

It soon became clear, however, that Montgomery was serious in his request, and the distressed Bedell Smith was forced to refer the matter to his chief who, when he also suggested that the whole matter was a joke, found himself very nearly in the position of being accused of bilking on a debt of honor. Under the circumstances, Eisenhower released a Flying Fortress complete with crew for Montgomery's personal use, but during talks with Brooke at Algiers let it be known that the whole matter had infuriated him.

To the end of his life, Montgomery insisted that Bedell Smith had made a serious bet and then tried to laugh his way out of it, but when asked what pledge he had offered against the Flying Fortress in the event that he did not reach Sousse, he said that the matter had never come up—which makes it difficult to see how a serious bet could have existed. But he did get his Flying Fortress, and Eisenhower, being the great gentleman he was, would appear to have fogiven him after his immediate rage had subsided.

The prime minister and the C.I.G.S. arrived back in London on June 5, content that the agreed strategy embodied at least a continuation of attacks upon Italy, but conscious now that they must prove to the Americans that their own determination upon a cross-Channel invasion equalled their Ally's. They immediately came up against even more evidence of the debilitating effects of Admiral King's diversion of shipping to the Pacific.

Sir Alan Brooke and Maj. Gen. Morgan, the senior planner for the invasion (now at last renamed Overlord) were both convinced that the initial landings must be made on a five-division front, with at least ten full-strength fighting divisions poised for a swift follow-up—and unless production of landing craft and their arrival in England was at least doubled during the next eight to ten months, this would be a logistic impossibility. Facts and figures sent to Washington were invariably referred to King as the highest naval authority, and they received scant attention from him. Efforts to underline the seriousness of the situation risked being interpreted as yet another British attempt to obstruct the operation.

But the planning went on despite all temptations to temporize, though after one intense session trying to reconcile minimum requirements with forecast availabilities, Brooke turned to Morgan and said, "Well, there it is. It won't work, but you must bloody well make it!" He then went off to visit Maj. Gen. Hobart, happily back training yet another armored division and designing specialized tanks to undertake the extraordinarily varied tasks required in landing a sea-borne force upon a hostile beach. Amphibious tanks were perhaps the most revolutionary of the new vehicles, but Hobart was now experimenting with tanks to scale sea walls, to belch flame and fire, to bulldoze through hedges and entanglements, to flail their way across mine fields, to carry bridges, to act as ramps for other tanks, and above all to guard the infantry during the crucial opening hours and days against enemy attempts to throw them back into the sea.

For Brooke, the next few weeks were a time of enormous activity, undertaken now with confidence that basically matters were going well. His Mediterranean strategy was at last accepted, the British command team that he had chosen during the dark days before Alamein had proved its worth, and cooperation with the main ally at least in Europe was satisfactory. He was optimistic enough to believe that in the end all problems would be solved.

He returned to London after a few days to tackle once again the mass of paperwork that always accumulated during even the briefest absence and on June 15 attended yet another war cabinet meeting. But before he went into the conference room, Mr. Churchill called him into his own office to make an electrifying suggestion. During the last few days, the prime minister told him, he had come to the conclusion that Sir Alan was the right man to take supreme command of Overlord when the invasion was launched. The Americans had held the command in North Africa, he said, and certainly exercised it in the Pacific, so he was sure that they would accept a British commander for operations launched from the British shores. It would be a fitting culmination to Sir Alan's military career, a just reward for his grueling labors of the last two years, and for his self-denial when he had refused active command in the Middle East.

Sir Alan would remain as C.I.G.S. until the end of the year and then take over command as soon as final plans for the gigantic operation had been agreed on. But in the meantime, the matter should be kept a secret between them both.

Throughout the morning of July 9, 1943, the invasion fleets steamed past Malta, those carrying the U.S. Seventh Army under the command of Lieutenant General George Patton on the west of the island, those carrying the British Eighth Army under Montgomery on the east. Twenty-five hundred ships and landing craft escorted or were carrying 160,000 men, 14,000 vehicles, 600 tanks, and 1,800 guns in what was to that date the largest amphibious operation in history, due within hours to enter waters heavily mined and possibly guarded by U-boats, threatened by the existence of large enemy battle fleets well within striking distance, as well as both German and Italian air squadrons operating from shore bases.

Upon reaching the shores of Sicily, the armies would storm open beaches, and in order to occupy the entire island, they would have to defeat an enemy force of nearly 300,000, of whom 40,000 were German veterans of the Fifteenth Panzer Grenadier Division and the Herman Göring Panzer Division.

During that day as the huge concourse of ships moved slowly past the island that had so recently come close to starvation, the wind rose steadily in a typical Mediterranen summer storm and by evening had reached gale force; aboard the crowded transports, sea sickness claimed victims at every rank, vomit slimed the heaving decks, and an overpowering stench filled the holds as the sailors fought their way between the sweating, groaning soldiers to help when they could and to work the ship all the time. Back at the headquarters in Malta, General Eisenhower watched the maps, listened to the weather reports and the advice from the naval staff, and at the crucial moment took his own counsel. Then he nodded; the operation would go on.

On crowded airfields in Tunisia, the engines of 109 American C-47s and 35 British Albemarles were being warmed up, their crews climbing aboard, while behind each plane was linked a Waco or Horsa glider packed with the 1,500 officers and men of the British First Airlanding Brigade. Just before 7:00 P.M. they began to take off. At first they flew into clear evening air, but by the time they were approaching Malta for their assembly and turning point the sky had darkened; they were into the gale center, and the winds were driving the planes off course, buffeting the gliders.

Seven tugs had failed even to reach the Tunisian coast; one towrope snapped, and another was accidentally released to send the gliders down into the sea; and two pilots over the Malta Channel lost both formation and their way, so they turned back to North Africa. But the remaining 133 tugs and gliders all assembled in due course above their final checkpoint—Cape Passero, the southeastern tip of Sicily. Against the inky sea the dark bulk of the land was hardly visible, and with all formation now gone and pilots flying their own courses, two more decided they were lost and turned back to North Africa.

The rest turned northeastward from the Cape, out over the seas again, the pilots desperately trying to find the glider release point off the eastern coast to the south of Syracuse. The wind blew some completely off course, and another twenty-five decided that the lives of the airborne troops were too valuable to risk and took them back to Tunisia; the other 115 released their tows, carrying now some 1,200 men.

More than half the tows dropped into the sea, and the majority of their cargoes drowned, even those who managed to scramble out of the ditched gliders being dragged under by the weight of their equipment in the heavy seas. Fifty-four gliders actually landed in Sicily, only twelve on or even near their designated landing grounds. Of the fifteen hundred men who had been dispatched to secure and hold the Ponte Grande over the River Cavadonna, just south of Syracuse, less than a hundred actually arrived.

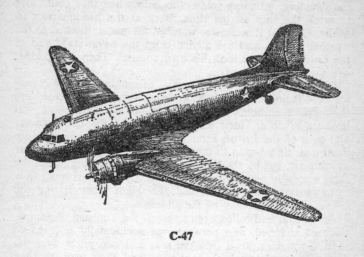

C-47

Two hours after the British airborne troops had taken off, another two hundred twenty-two C-47s filled with 3,400 American paratroopers took off from Tunisian airfields, the majority to fly low over the sea in the mistaken premise that visibility would be better at low altitudes. Windshields obscured by salt, they lost direction, missed checkpoints, and approached Sicily from all directions and only by luck at the correct place. Two pilots gave up and returned to North Africa, one crashed into the sea, and as the majority approached the Sicilian coastline, antiaircraft fire rose at them from the towns and ports on the southwestern shore along the stretch that formed the main objective for the U.S. Seventh Army. It seemed that the defenses were alert.

By now the simple objective of every pilot was to release his paratroops over land—never mind about the correct dropping zones, just avoid dropping them into the sea! Of the whole of Brig. Gen. James Gavin's command, only two hundred were anywhere near their objective at dawn, the rest being scattered over southeastern Sicily while their commander himself believed for some hours that he had been dropped into mainland Italy.

All the C-47s had turned back toward North Africa by 10:00 P.M., and those that had not been shot down by antiaircraft fire or ditched because of mechanical failure were back at their bases well before midnight. About an hour before midnight the wind died away even more quickly than it had risen, and the ships carrying the Eighth Army were approaching their landing beaches more or less on time. Those bearing the Seventh Army had further to go and still had the remnants of the gale blowing on the southwestern shores to cope with, so they were about an hour late.

As the Italian units along the stretch between Cape Passero and Syracuse had decided that no one in their senses would attempt a seaborne landing in such weather and had relaxed their attention once the Allied aircraft had flown off, the first waves of the British assault landed without opposition and swept over the coastal defenses almost before their presence was noticed. Belatedly, a few inland artillery units opened fire on the invasion beaches, to be immediately blanketed with shells from one or more of the six battleships—*Nelson, Rodney, Warspite, Valiant, Howe and King George V*—that had accompained the force for just this purpose.

Shortly after dawn on July 10, advanced units of the British Fifth Division were approaching Casibile and by 8:00 A.M. the town was in their hands, the whole of XIII Corps were coming ashore to the south of them, while the Fifty-first Highland Division and the First Canadian Division of XXX Corps with Royal Marine Commandos on their western flank were ashore around the corner of Cape Passero, between the point and Pozallo.

Further to the west, the U.S. Seventh Army had not been quite so fortunate. The coastal defenders had not been asleep along their stretch, and the ships and landing craft came under fire from almost the moment of their arrival. Again,

fire from the heavy naval guns soon obliterated most of the opposition much to General Patton's astonishment and delight, as he had placed little reliance in naval assurances, but the pier at Gela, which would have been very useful for a quick buildup, was blown to pieces by demolition charges as two Ranger battalions were actually sailing for it; and by 4:30 A.M. Italian and German aircraft were over the crowded beaches to sink two transports in awkward positions.

But by mid-morning all the forward strike formations of both Eighth and Seventh Armies were ashore and probing inland, the latter suddenly to receive an unexpected bonus; if their airborne colleagues were not in exactly the right positions, they had coagulated during darkness into twenty or thirty independent groups and were creating chaos in the country just behind the landing beaches, cutting communications, ambushing lone cars, trucks, or even small convoys, attacking crossroad guard posts, and on one occasion holding up an entire Italian mobile regiment that had been sent to find out what was happening at Gela.

But by mid-afternoon, at the other end of the invasion beaches, the tiny British airborne force that had taken the Ponte Grande was in desperate straits. Eight officers and sixty-five men had first taken the bridge in darkness, but attempts to push them off it had begun shortly after dawn and hardly slackened throughout the morning. Italian soldiers, marines, and sailors had been sent out from Syracuse in ever-stronger waves, and by three o'clock all but fifteen of the defenders had been killed or wounded, and ammunition was running low. At three-thirty a massed assault overran the survivors, but eight managed to escape and as the British had removed all the demolition charges while in possession of the bridge, the Italian marines had now to try to emplace some more. Two of the escaping eight therefore took position halfway up an overlooking hill and from there sniped at every movement on the bridge, while the remaining six, stumbling with exhaustion, made their way south toward Casibile. Three miles along the road they met a mobile column from the Fifth Division, which they led back to the bridge, which fell immediately into British hands again, and by five o'clock the column was driving into Syracuse.

By the end of the first day, the British held the coastal strip from Pozzallo around to Syracuse. This vital port was sufficiently undamaged for immediate use. The American Seventh

Army held nearly forty miles of beach between Scoglitti and Licata, while scattered bands of marauding British and American airborne troops were loose all over the southern half of the island.

It was not to be expected that matters would continue quite so smoothly for the Allies, especially with two highly efficient panzer divisions deployed against them, but the next few days saw the satisfactory development of the overall plan. The Eighth Army consolidated and began their advance up the eastern coast toward Messina, the Seventh drove north alongside, aiming for the northern coast near San Stephano, at the same time guarding the inner flank of British advance.

Within ten days the Canadians had reached Enna in the center of the island, and two days later Patton's troops had not only reached the north coast but had turned west and occupied Palermo, taking prisoner thousands of Italian soldiers more than happy to stop fighting. The Americans were welcomed everywhere by delighted Sicilians to whom quite a number of the soldiers were related.

And by then, the political situation in Italy was taking a dramatic turn, which seemed likely to influence the whole course of the war.

The Italian people had never been enthusiastic about the war, finding themselves from the start fighting with inadequate weapons against an enemy they did not hate, yoked to an ally for whom they felt no particular affection. Before El Alamein the majority had hoped that their country might emerge from the conflict at least as well off and influential as when Mussolini took them in, but after Alamein and the unbroken succession of defeats since, they knew that the best they could hope for was defeat at the hands of a kindly enemy, at worst the total devastation of their country.

And if they were to avoid this last fate, then the regime that had ruled their country for twenty-one years must go.

Dissatisfaction with the military control of the war—which Mussolini had assumed from the moment he decided that Italy must earn her place at the peace table when England and France had been beaten—had grown during the long retreat across Africa, and with the Allied landings on Sicily, it appeared openly in every circle including even the Fascist hierarchy itself. As for the army, the new chief of staff,

General Vittorio Ambrosio, who had been appointed early in the year, made no secret of his belief that it lacked every military necessity from artillery to boots for the infantry, and most of all, any vestige of sound morale.

Mussolini and Hitler had made a habit of meeting at fairly regular intervals, and faced with the hard reality of the successful Allied landings in Sicily, Hitler called for an immediate conference. It took place on July 17 in a villa near Feltre, some fifty miles north of Venice, and on his way there Mussolini agreed with Ambrosio that he must tell Hitler of Italy's desperate need for an armistice and their wish for withdrawal from the Pact of Steel.

He was given little chance. Hitler announced that he could only spare one day from the Russian front, and as his usual interpretation of the term conference was of a gathering that listened sycophantically to everything he had to say, he occupied the whole of the three-hour session. He explained the course of the war to date and his immediate plans to stem the reverses that had recently plagued them all. He complained that the Italian army was inadequate at every level from commander in chief down to private soldier. His suggested remedy for this was the immediate appointment of a German general to reform and command the Italian army—under Mussolini. Sicily, he said, must be turned into another Stalingrad!

There was a brief break for lunch, which the two delegations took separately. Ambrosio and Bastianini of the foreign office pressed Mussolini to keep to their agreement and use the only time left—the journey by car back to the airfield where Hitler's plane waited and which the two dictators would share alone—to make it clear to Hitler that Italy must get out of the war. Il Duce promised to do this, but one look at both faces when the dictators emerged from the car revealed that nothing of the sort had occurred; Mussolini had, in fact, merely accepted Hitler's suggestion of a German commander in chief, to buttress his own position.

They arrived back in Rome to discover that during their absence some seven hundred Allied planes had bombed the capital. Marshaling yards had been very badly hit, and millions of leaflets had been dropped explaining the dire state of their country and the available remedies for the condition to a thoroughly demoralized populace, most of whom were eagerly collecting and reading them.

That evening Mussolini actually drafted a letter to Hitler setting out the true position, but it was not sent, and when it became obvious that he would never break with Hitler himself, the members of the Fascist Grand Council, which had not met for three and a half years, decided it was time to take action themselves. A meeting was convened for the evening of July 24, and one of the members, Dino Grandi, who had in the past been one of Mussolini's closest friends and supporters, proposed that military power should immediately revert to the Crown and that all the established governing bodies should be allowed to function as had been intended, and not controlled solely by the whim of one man. In a scene not unlike the one that had taken place three years before in the House of Commons, he turned to Il Duce and said:

"It is not enough that you assume the responsibility. We are also in it, and so is the country. Among the many absurd and empty phrases you caused to be written on walls all over Italy is one you pronounced in 1924 from the balcony of the Palazzo Chigi; 'May all factions perish! May even our own perish—provided the nation lives!' Well, now is come the time for your faction to perish!"

The vote was finally taken at about two in the morning, and to Mussolini's discomfiture, nineteen members supported Grandi's motion and only nine were against. "Then there is no more to be said," Mussolini announced as he got to his feet. "The session is over. Gentlemen, you have provoked the crisis of the regime."

But after a few hours sleep, he had sufficiently recovered his spirits to believe that when he took the results of the Grand Council vote to the king that evening, Victor Emmanual would just refuse to accept it and order him to deal with the matter as he thought best.

But it was not like that at all. The king received him quite warmly, but when he reported the Grand Council vote, His Majesty nodded, indicated that he supported it too, and was quite sure that both the army and the Italian people would be delighted when they heard the news. A shocked and astonished Duce was then led out into the courtyard, where he was promptly arrested and driven away in an ambulance. The next day a new government was formed, headed by the venerable and lifelong anti-Fascist, Marshal Badoglio, with a Cabinet that did not include a single member of the Fascist Party. Twenty-one years of dictatorship were at an end.

* * *

The effect of the successes in Sicily on strategic thinking in both London and Washington, followed now by the downfall of Mussolini, seemed at first all that Sir Alan Brooke and his British colleagues could have hoped for. As early as July 18 Eisenhower had cabled his recommendation that as soon as Messina was in Allied hands, Brooke should be allowed to cross the Straits and put an army onto mainland Italy, coupled with a suggestion that if the British undertook that operation, the Americans should put a force ashore in Salerno Bay nearly two hundred miles to the north, thus helping to secure for Allied use the port of Naples and also to cut off the Axis forces to the south.

To Brooke's astonishment, both Marshall and King agreed to both suggestions with some enthusiasm, which sent Mr. Churchill into transports of delight.

"Why crawl up the leg like a harvest bug from the ankle upwards?" he asked. "Let us rather strike at the knee!"

When the news of Mussolini's downfall reached Churchill, his vision began to range much farther up the thigh of the Italian peninsula. Would it not be possible to strike up as far as Rome—or even higher if the Italians could be persuaded not to resist—in the hope that the Germans, presented with a fait accompli, might accept that the Austrian border was the line for them to defend?

And what about the Balkans? Yugoslav partisans were already a formidable force there, a great deal of subversive activity was smoldering in Greece, and surely now was the time for swift exploitation in the Aegean, where the Italian garrisons in the Cyclades and especially the Dodecanese might be encouraged not only to welcome Allied forces, but also to turn their arms on their late allies. On July 27 Mr. Churchill called for plans for the occupation of Rhodes and was cheered to find that Maitland Wilson (who had taken command of the Middle East when Alexander became deputy commander, North Africa) had available for the task one infantry division, two armored regiments, and a parachute battalion. All that was missing was the transport to take the troops to Rhodes and the necessary air cover.

This was the problem everywhere. Even Salerno was only just within air cover from Sicily, while for a series of operations further away, the Allies would need far more

aircraft carriers than were available in the Mediterranean—
as many, indeed, as Admiral King had sent to the Pacific. As
for landing craft, many of those used in the Sicily landings
were being repaired in various North African ports, and the
bulk of the remainder were in use supplying the fighting
divisions—but at least one step could be taken to help. Very
promptly the British Chiefs of Staff issued a "stand-still
order," which had the immediate effect of freezing in Alexandria and the Levantine ports three Landing Ships Infantry
(LSI) and several Landing Ships Tank (LST) intended for
early dispatch to the Bay of Bengal for the operations against
Ramree and Akyab. In view of the promise opening before
the Allies from Corsica to the Dardanelles, this seemed to
them the most intelligent course to pursue.

It was thus with astonishment and despair that both the
British Chiefs of Staff and the American generals in the Mediterranean received instructions from Washington to the
effect that the schedule agreed at Trident for the return of
aircraft, experienced fighting divisions, and landing and assault craft to the United Kingdom must be strictly adhered
to, and none of it retained in the Mediterranean area, however
inviting the opportunities that might arise there.

As it happened agreement had been reached at the Trident
conference that events that summer might move so fast that
another conference would soon be needed, so it seemed that
early opportunity for discussion and revision of outdated
plans was possible. Arrangements for Quadrant, to be held in
Quebec, were already well advanced, and by August 5, Mr.
Churchill and his usual party were again aboard the *Queen
Mary*, arriving on August 10 to find that Mr. Roosevelt
would not be leaving Washington for a few days, but that a
large American contingent was already there. The British
soon found, however, that the Americans were unanimous in
their determination that this time their own strategy of a
direct thrust at the heart of Nazi Germany would prevail,
with no Mediterranean diversions acting as a suction pump to
draw men and material away from the main effort.

The Americans felt themselves in a strong position. Their
production of war material was reaching its peak, shipping
construction was more than keeping step with losses, MacAr-
thur's campaigns in the Pacific were all succeeding, and now
Patton's army was sweeping all before it in Sicily. As for the
immediate future, the only obstacle to the full implementa-

tion of American strategy would be British obstinacy, probably inspired by their political, almost colonial, ambitions in the Balkans, and for this no American soldier or sailor had the slightest patience, and they were confident that their president shared their views.

Nonetheless, it was with some misgiving that they discovered that Mr. Churchill was leaving Quebec two days after his arrival, to spend until August 15 with Mr. Roosevelt at the presidential home at Hyde Park.

They need not have worried; Mr. Stimson had got there first.

The American secretary of war had in fact just completed a tour of American troops and bases in both England and North Africa and during his travels had neither registered nor absorbed anything that might contradict his preconceived notions. During World War I Churchill had diverted military effort from the western front and sent it off on dangerous entanglements in the eastern Mediterranean; ergo, he was trying to do the same again now. To Mr. Stimson, the British prime minister was a dangerous opportunist who neither wished to form a long-term plan nor keep to one unless compelled, and Brooke was his lap dog who merely echoed his master's words.

In the old man's eyes it almost seemed that the fall of Mussolini and the defection of Italy from the Axis posed greater dangers to the Allied victory than if they had remained loyal to the Pact of Steel, for such events fueled Britain's desire to stay in the Mediterranean and avoid the only course that would bring victory to the Allies—the gigantic clash of arms with the Wehrmacht across the English Channel.

In Africa Mr. Stimson embarrassed General Eisenhower, who could see the opportunities opening before him but could not argue too forcibly for their exploitation without running the risk of being labeled pro-Limey in the top echelons of his own government and thus almost certainly losing their confidence; and no words in favor of the British argument were heard by the secretary of war, no evidence that his suspicions might be unjustified was recognized as such.

There were none so blind as Mr. Stimson in the summer of 1943, and upon his return to Washington his report to Mr.

Roosevelt rang with such phrases as "The difference between us is a vital difference of faith. . . . Only by massing the immense vigour and power of the American and British nations . . . can the War be brought to a real victory. . . . The British theory (which cropped up again and again in unguarded sentences of the British leaders.) . . . series of attritions in Northern Italy, in the eastern Mediterranean, in Greece, in the Balkans, in Rumania." And one of the most crucial passages read:

> We cannot now rationally hope to be able to cross the Channel and come to grips with our German enemy under a British commander. His Prime Minister and his Chief of the Imperial General Staff are frankly at variance with such a proposal. The shadows of Passchendaele and Dunquerque still hang too heavily over the imagination of these leaders of his Government. Though they have rendered lip-service to the operation, their hearts are not in it and it will require more independence, more faith, and more vigour than it is reasonable to expect we can find in any British commander to overcome the natural difficulties of such an operation carried on in such an atmosphere of his government.

His report concluded with the strongest recommendations that Mr. Roosevelt should insist upon General Marshall being appointed supreme commander for Overlord. And Mr. Roosevelt accepted it, together with practically all Mr. Stimson's opinions and theories for future action; and in respect of that future action, the president also deemed it essential that not only should Operation Overlord have an American commander, it must also have a lot more American troops; Operation Bolero must be stepped up.

On the whole, Mr. Churchill was not gravely disappointed when he found that there was nothing that even he could do to change the president's mind. True, he would have to break the news to Sir Alan Brooke that he would not, after all, command Overlord, but he knew his C.I.G.S. well enough by now to know that Sir Alan would accept the disappointment with soldierly dignity. And the arrival of more American divisions in the United Kingdom would at least insure greater strength in the invasion and thus less chance of failure.

By some means or other the prime minister divined that

Mr. Roosevelt would not allow General Marshall to stray so far from his side, and that General Eisenhower instead would command the invasion force—which would leave the Mediterranean with a vacant appointment to be filled. Moreover, Mr. Churchill felt strongly that a British supreme commander should be appointed for Southeast Asia (Burma, Indonesia, Malaya), and the appointment of an American commander to Overlord would give him bargaining strength in both these matters. To exchange Brooke as supremo in England, for Alexander as supremo in the Mediterranean and Mountbatten as supremo in the Indian Ocean would surely not be unacceptable.

By the time prime minister and president arrived in Quebec, there seemed to be no great differences of opinion still to be resolved between them.

There were also not such vast differences of opinion between the American and British Chiefs of Staff as the former expected, and the ease with which the Americans seemed to be winning their arguments in the early days of the conference left them feeling somewhat suspicious.

General Marshall, as convinced as Stimson that the British thought the Axis could be defeated without a cross-Channel invasion, warned his colleagues, "We must go into this argument in the spirit of winning." Thus the Americans' opening blow was an aggressive accusation that in issuing the "standstill order" in the Mediterranean, the British had unilaterally abrogated a firm decision taken at Trident. No consideration of the way Admiral King had been at least bending some of the decisions also taken there entered their minds, and in the atmosphere generated by their argumentative truculence it was possible as well that the British refrained from mentioning it, too.

The next target for the American onslaught concerned the agenda for the conference as proposed by the British, which placed discussion of post-Husky operations at the top; the Americans felt these so irrelevant and unimportant that in their agenda they came seventh, preceded by such matters as overall strategic concept, operations in Europe—with Overlord and the bombing offensive as priority—submarine warfare, and future employment of French forces.

They then sat back and braced themselves for the counterattack to come and were thus slightly bemused when the British put up almost no suggestions for change, Sir Alan Brooke stating that no one on the British side had any wish to tamper with the main strategic decisions already taken at both Washington and Casablanca, i.e., that the defeat of the Axis powers in Europe should be brought about as soon as possible by a successful attack across the English Channel; in which respect perhaps the conference would like to see the latest plans brought over for Operation Overlord by Lt. Gen. Sir Frederick Morgan, upon which he and his staff had been working hard for the last six months?

But did not the British wish to divert significant military effort to Italy and the Balkans? Only, replied Sir Alan, in sufficient force to attract enough German divisions away from northern France to give Overlord the greatest chance of success.

This was enough to start a whole catalog of arguments, which went on with varying acerbity until the afternoon of August 16, when Sir Alan, who was chairman of this conference as it was on Commonwealth soil, suggested another off the record talk between the Chiefs of Staff only.

They were not going to get anywhere, he told them all, unless they stopped distrusting each other. The Americans doubted the real intentions of the British to put their full hearts into the cross-Channel operation in the spring of 1944, and the British felt that the Americans would insist upon rigid adherence to plans agreed in the past, despite events or developments that might render them inapplicable or even irrelevant.

The British were fully commited to Overlord, he assured them, but felt that its success would depend not so much on the total force that the Allies could assemble, as on the relative strengths that would be ranged against each other at the actual time and place of the landings. In the assessment and adjustment of those relative forces, flexibility of mind, thought, and action would be an essential ingredient.

That afternoon session served to clear the air to a great extent as General Marshall accepted Sir Alan's assurances on Overlord; but an atmosphere seemed still to pervade the talks that the Americans suspected the British would try to avoid an issue somewhere, perhaps along the difficult line between being flexible and being "downright flabby!" As a result, although they agreed to inserting into the final conference conclusions regarding the European theater some phraseology admitting the possible advantages of a spirit of opportunism, they insisted upon cancellation of the stand-still order on shipping and landing craft in the Mediterranean, and a reaffirmation of the transfer of the seven experienced divisions of Eisenhower's command to the United Kingdom by November 1, 1943.

In this regard, the Americans themselves had some figures to put forward. According to their calculations, the dispatch of those seven divisions would still leave in the Mediterranean theater some twenty-four divisions for offensive purposes. Of these, ten could undoubtedly be profitably used maintaining pressure on the German forces stationed in Italy. The remaining ten Anglo-American divisions plus the four newly equipped French divisions would therefore be used, when the appropriate moment came, for an invasion of southern France, which would drive northward and thus act directly in that diversion of opposition to the cross-Channel invasion, upon which Sir Alan Brooke and his colleagues were so insistent.

Where they—and the shipping that would be needed to transport them—would in no circumstances be used, would be in Greece, Yugoslavia, or the Aegean.

CHAPTER ELEVEN

The Badoglio government lasted for forty-five days, and it is impossible not to feel some sympathy for the marshal and his colleagues in the predicament in which they found themselves.

They and the whole Italian population wanted to get out of the war, but were realistic enough to know that there was a price to be paid. The Allied armies were in Sicily, and obviously the occupation of the island by them was but a matter of days away, but German divisions were on the Italian mainland itself, better equipped and far more strongly motivated than the Italian formations alongside them. Obviously some part of the Italian mainland would shortly become a battlefield, but what could the new government do to insure that the area devastated by war would be kept to a minimum?

Obviously, they must play for time, and they must also maneuver with consummate diplomacy and delicacy. Put more bluntly, the marshal's position was perhaps best summed up by Mr. Churchill's comment "Badoglio knows that he is going to doublecross someone—and let us ensure that it is the Germans, not us!"

The process had begun on the evening Badoglio took power (July 25) when he announced that he and his country would continue the fight alongside their German comrades until the Allies were beaten, at the same time instructing the Italian counsellor at the Lisbon embassy to make contact with the British ambassador to suggest that the Allied governments should not take this announcement too seriously.

This piece of Machiavellianism set the tone for the rest of the month. During the days that followed, there took place a sequence of devious moves by all parties concerned (including the Germans who had little doubt of the new Italian government's real intentions), and as a result of these—coupled with several heavy bombing raids on targets in southern Italy—a short armistice was signed in an olive grove near Syracuse on September 3. Under its terms all Italian air and ground forces would lay down their arms when approached by Allied soldiers, the Italian fleet would sail for Malta, Allied prisoners of war in Italian hands would be released and in no circumstances allowed to fall into German hands, and all Italian territory including the Mediterranean islands would be made available to the Allies as operational bases from which to continue the war against the remaining European enemy.

For this the Allies were willing to guarantee "kindly and sympathetic treatment" to the Italians, and they also gave the Badoglio government the impression that they were contemplating an early landing on the Italian coast north of Rome with, in addition, an airborne division dropped onto the Rome airfields—and would react very favorably if Italian troops in the area attacked German units nearby at the same time. And the Allies also agreed that they would not announce the signing of the armistice to the world for nine days.

Badoglio and his colleagues were thus seriously discomfited both when General Eisenhower announced the terms of Italy's surrender four days early on the evening of September 8 and when the following morning Lt. Gen. Mark Clark's Fifth Army stormed ashore in Salerno Bay, south of Naples and nearly one hundred and fifty miles short of Rome, where German troops acting with their customary efficiency were already disarming the Italian units in the neighborhood and moving in some force into every commanding position.

Eighth Army formations had already crossed the Straits of Messina onto the toe of Italy on the morning the armistice had been signed, while other British formations sailed for the port of Taranto, which they captured against only the slightest opposition on September 9. Although it took until September 20 for all three groups to join up, by the end of the month the Allies were in possession of Naples on the west coast, Termoli on the east and thus, with the countryside between and to the south also in their hand, most of the foot of Italy. The long drive up the peninsula had begun, and no part of the Italian mainland was to escape the horrors of war.

King Victor Emmanuel and his family, together with Marshal Badoglio and the other members of his government, had managed to escape on the evening of September 9, from

Rome to Pescara, where they were picked up by an Allied corvette and taken to safety in the south. On the same day the Italian battle fleet duly sailed from their northern port for Malta, where they arrived the following day having lost the battleship *Roma* by Luftwaffe bombing en route. On the morning of September 11 a cable from Admiral Cunningham arrived at Whitehall informing the lordships of the admiralty that "the Italian battle fleet now lies at anchor under the guns of the fortress of Malta."

Some of the fruits of Sir Alan Brooke's Mediterranean policy were therefore being plucked; but there were still others on the branch.

Had it been left to the German generals in Berlin and Italy, drastic military action would have been taken in the peninsula immediately after Mussolini was overthrown. For many months at all levels of the German command it had been realized that their Italian ally was eager to quit the conflict, and German units had been moving into tactically advantageous positions between the Alps and Messina since the beginning of the year.

The generals were restrained from immediate action, however, on Hitler's direct orders, for he had concentrated the bulk of his armor and his most experienced divisions on the Russian front and could not quickly transfer them. He also seems to have allowed an unusual spirit of optimism to color his normally ruthless clarity of vision, hoping perhaps that with a little patient maneuvering, Il Duce could be put back into power. Surely after over twenty years, true Fascism could not be swept away so easily—and anyway Badoglio might prove to be another Pétain; it would certainly be easier to control Italy through a puppet government than by outright military occupation.

He agreed, however, that plans already in existence for the reinforcement of German forces in both Italy and the Balkans should be brought up to date and circulated to the relevant commands, and as it happened, the final version of the plans for Operation Axis went out on August 30. Just over a week later and thirty-five minutes after Eisenhower's broadcast of the terms of the short armistice had put an end to Hitler's hopes, the plans were put into action, and by the following morning the Apennine Passes were under German control, Italian air and military formations were being informed that they could either place themselves immediately under German command or lay down their arms and become prisoners, and what panzer units there were in Italy were racing for the northern ports—too late, as it happened, to catch the main prize.

In the south the German divisions evacuated from Sicily were already regrouping with others in the area to repel the next Allied thrust, wherever it might strike, and they quickly and efficiently disarmed every Italian unit in the area, not bothering to offer them an alternative that they felt would not be strictly honored even if accepted.

Such action and such efficiency were repeated elsewhere, notably in the Aegean Islands. Hitler was only too well aware of the value to the Third Reich of the Balkans and of the ring of islands that protected them. Not only were supplies of bauxite, copper, and chrome provided from the area, but German control kept bases out of Allied hands from which the Ploesti oil fields and indeed parts of the Reich heartland itself could easily be bombed; and there was always the thought that if the Dodecanese Islands in particular fell to the Allies, the pressure on Turkey to climb down off the fence on their side might prove irresistable.

There was also by the end of August another reason for holding on in the Aegean, in July the greatest tank battle in history, the Battle of Kursk had been fought, and since the beginning of August the whole world had watched the Russian counterattacks first wipe out the salients the panzers had gouged out of the Kursk bulge, then force the Wehrmacht back on each side until it was obvious that the much-vaunted Summer Offensive of 1943 had turned into a retreat —and German forces must not be seen to be pulling back on all fronts. In the Mediterranean at least, the lines must be held—in Italy as far south as possible and farther east, along the "Iron Ring" of protective islands, Kithera, Crete, Scarpanto, and especially Rhodes with its airfields at Marizza, Calato, and Cattavia from which all traffic up into the Aegean could be harried and all islands to the north dominated.

Mr. Churchill's valuation of the Aegean islands almost exactly coincided with Hitler's, and as has been shown, he had begun pressing for the invasion of Rhodes even before the end of July. Maitland Wilson was more than prepared to provide the forces, and by mid-August the Eighth Indian Division was training in amphibious operations along the Suez Canal, while an armored brigade collected new Sherman tanks and assembled at Haifa and Beirut. Paratroops were briefed to drop onto Marizza airfield, while the tanks once ashore would drive from the nearby coast to take Calato, and commandos would storm Cattavia, the whole operational schedule aimed toward a target date of mid-September.

Then on August 26, while some units were actually practicing loading and offloading exercises on the three LSIs, thirteen LSTs, and the headquarter ship, a coldly worded order arrived from the Combined Chiefs of Staff in Washington stating that the stand-still order, which had held the shipping in the Mediterranean had been cancelled, and all the landing craft and the headquarter ship must be released immediately to proceed to the Bay of Bengal in order to take part in the Arakan operations, some time in late 1943 or early 1944, for which they had been originally designated. Mr. Stimson had won.

Shorty afterwards orders arrived transferring the Eighth Indian Division to the central Mediterranean, so by the end of August there was little real striking power left in the area to take advantage of whatever opportunities were offered by Italy's defection from the Axis.

But what there was, was to be used to the fullest.

Admiral Campioni, the Italian governor of Rhodes, first heard the news of the Italian armistice from the wife of a German officer on the island, who telephoned him shortly after General Eisenhower's broadcast. Before he had much time to react, however, an officer from the staff of General Klemann, the commander of *Sturm Division Rhodos,* requested an interview with him during which it was agreed that the 35,000 Italian and 8,000 German troops on the island should all for the moment remain where they were—an arrangement to which Campioni had little choice but to agree as the Italian troops were chronically short of transport. Not so the Germans, who used the respite thus given them to send strong patrols out to the three airfields in an effort to take them over. They met some determined opposition at Marizza, where the Italian artillery, as so often during the Second

World War, proved far more courageous and efficient than they have been given credit for.

The remainder of Klemann's command concentrated around the town of Rhodes itself, deploying their artillery to command the port entrance and the approaches along the two main roads. That night the island was shrouded in a most unseasonable fog, which concealed the movements of the clear-minded and purposeful Germans, but added to the bewilderment of most of the rest of the island's inhabitants; by morning German troops dominated all key positions except around Marizza airfield.

Admiral Campioni spent an uncomfortable day, still in ignorance of the steps that his new government might or might not want him to take, but acutely aware that General Klemann was watching his every move. Some members of his staff felt that he should strongly protest the blatant breaking of the agreement by the Germans and order them to return to their original positions; others, himself included, felt that without far more military power and efficiency at his command, there was little point in making what Klemann would know was an empty gesture. There were still reports coming in of sporadic fighting around Marizza in the late evening, but none of Campioni's problems seemed any nearer a solution when he went to bed.

He was awakened at about half past one in the morning by an excited member of his staff with the news that he had unexpected visitors. Hastily donning a dressing gown, he went down to meet them. In the hall below he found Major the Earl Jellicoe and a British sergeant who refused to be parted from his signal set. Lying on a stretcher and being attended by one of his own doctors was a Major Dolbey, who had broken a leg upon landing on the hard perimeter track at Marizza (it had been his first parachute jump) and was to act as interpreter. They had come from Egypt to find out Admiral Campioni's attitude to the recent events at home, the degree to which he wished to rid himself and the island of the German presence, and the steps to this end of which the Italian garrison was capable. Major Jellicoe had brought with him a personal letter from General Maitland Wilson assuring Admiral Campioni of British sympathy in his predicament, but believing himself in danger of being caught by hostile troops, Jellicoe had eaten it shortly after landing and was suffering as a result from nausea and acute thirst.

The physical needs of the British visitors having been satisfied, a discussion now took place reminiscent of the presumed conversation between Northumberland and Stanley before Bosworth Field. The Italians, Admiral Campioni assured Major Jellicoe, would be delighted to be rid of the Germans. But whereas the Italians were dispersed around the island the Germans were concentrated, whereas the Italians were poorly armed the Germans had both armor and artillery at their disposal, and whereas the Italians were immobile through lack of transport the Germans could go anywhere they liked on the island at great speed.

But of course, the immediate landing of a British armored division augmented by extra artillery and perhaps preceded by a strong airborne drop onto Marizza would change the entire situation. Not only would such a force meet with no resistance at all in Italian-controlled areas, it would be welcomed and indeed could rely upon guidance, logistic support, and aid behind their lines as they advanced against the German positions, as well as active support from the Italian artillery, perhaps also from some of the infantry units—especially if the British brought extra arms for them. The admiral's staff nodded eagerly at all their chief's main points, and there was a suggestion that even more Italian enthusiasm than he was promising would encourage the British formations as they swarmed ashore.

They were thus somewhat dismayed when Jellicoe informed them that only small bodies of parachutists and commandos could arrive for six days at least, and when pressed, he could give only the vaguest assurances as to the size and armament of whatever larger forces would arrive after that. The admiral thereupon became glum and rather petulant, but he agreed to the use of the naval wireless station by the sergeant to contact Cairo, thus conserving his own batteries, and placed a room, beds, and the continuing service of his doctor at his guests' disposal. He then retired to his own room after earnestly begging Jellicoe to don civilian clothing and not to show himself around the castle more than necessary.

Little more occurred during the night, but when daylight came, the continual passage through the castle of German officers played on everybody's nerves, and at one time during an air raid alert, Sergeant Kesterton narrowly avoided leaping into a shelter with one of Klemann's senior staff officers.

During the afternoon, the British attempted to catch up on lost sleep but were awakened shortly after five o'clock by an agitated Campioni with the news that Klemann had now obviously received orders from higher command and had informed him that German forces were about to take over full control of Rhodes and move into the castle itself; and at the slightest sign of resistance from the Italians, he would shell the town and all headquarter installations. The British must leave the island immediately, Campioni announced, and he suggested that any of the small bodies of parachutists or commandos who might be on their way should turn back, or perhaps aside, and land instead on one of the neighboring islands less heavily garrisoned by Germans.

There was little Jellicoe could do but agreed, so shortly after dark, a small but peculiar party left the castle dressed in civilian clothes that had obviously not been tailored for them, taking with them maps of both the island defenses and the Aegean mine fields (which proved dangerously inaccurate), several bottles of wine, and a picnic basket. At the port they embarked in an Italian MAS boat and set off for the neighboring island of Casteloriso, which, as Jellicoe well knew, had been occupied the previous morning by members of the Long Range Desert Group and of the Special Boat Service—the raiding formation he himself commanded.

They arrived early on the morning of September 11 to find that the senior officer of the whole expedition, Brigadier Turnbull, had already left in accordance with previous arrangements, taking the main body of the force—some fifty men—to the island of Simi, from whence it had been agreed that they would descend on Rhodes itself. Snatching a quick breakfast, Jellicoe hurried after Turnbull to inform him of the latest developments, accompanied by one of Campioni's senior staff officers, Colonel Fanetza, who Campioni had sent along as evidence of his own good faith.

The colonel, however, was a less cooperative man than he had allowed himself to appear, and while Jellicoe slept aboard the MAS, he ordered the *tenente* in charge to return to Casteloriso, explaining his decision when Jellicoe awoke with tales of a radio message from Campioni received en route. How true the story was will probably never be known, but with the return to Casteloriso came the news that Campioni had formally capitulated to Klemann—and Rhodes with its vital airfields was now under complete German control.

* * *

But there were other islands in the Dodecanese where Italian resistance might prove more—or German determination less—than on Rhodes, and during those early days of September 1943, the officers and men of the raiding forces visited them and in many cases left small parties both to reorganize and to stiffen Italian resistance against whatever German aggression might in due course show itself. Simi, Stampalia, and Icaria all received such support, and on Cos, Leros, and Samos the raiding forces made arrangements—with the eager cooperation of the Italian garrisons—for the reception of much larger British forces as soon as shipping could be found for them.

Most of the troops were to be brought up either in Royal Navy destroyers or in caiques crewed by their Greek owners acting under charter or by the motley collection of amateur sailors commanded by Lt. Comm. Adrian Seligman and given the slightly raffish title of the Levant Schooner Flotilla. By the end of September, nearly five thousand men of the 234th Infantry Brigade had been brought up, many left at Casteloriso, over 2,000 taken to Leros and Samos, while the rest including some paratroops and men of the RAF Regiment were on Cos, the only island apart from Rhodes that possesed a workable fighter airstrip. From it were operating the Spitfires of No. 7 South African Air Force Squadron, while extra air cover in the area was provided somewhat sporadically by Liberators and cannon-firing Mitchell bombers operating from Cyprus. In addition, some delay to German intentions was provided by another thirty-eight Liberators from the U.S. Northwest Africa Strategic Air Force, who bombed all three of the Rhodes airfields.

It was upon the Royal Navy that perhaps the greatest burden fell during these days. Not only were destroyers the only ships able to carry out rapid sorties into and out of the danger area in the hours of darkness, but they were the only ones capacious enough to carry vehicles or artillery—and only jeeps and light antiaircraft guns such as Bofors guns at that. As they were also intended to carry out marauding sweeps to catch convoys supplying the German garrison on Rhodes, they were very busy indeed and their losses inevitable—two destroyers were sunk in one day after a run to Leros.

Caique

With such activity throughout the area, it was not long before the Germans became aware of the British buildup, and once they had consolidated their hold on Rhodes, they turned their attention to Cos, the only island from which Allied aircraft could threaten their control of the Aegean. Stuka bombing by Junkers 88s began on September 17, with the airfield at Antimachia the main target and other temporary strips laid at Lambia and Marmari by the toiling RAF Regiment attacked soon afterwards. For the rest of the month, both RAF and the men of the First Battalion the Durham Light Infantry (DLI) sweated day and night filling in the craters or diving for cover as Me 109 fighter escorts swept in strafing as Stukas pulled away. Most of the DLIs had spent the last few months in Malta during the Luftwaffe's recent blitz, and they knew both the dangers of air attacks and the best techniques to avoid them, but this early resumption of life lived under the howl of Stukas, the crash of bombs, and the chatter of machine guns did nothing for their morale. Neither did days spent filling holes and digging slit trenches train them for repelling an invasion, which by the end of the month was obviously imminent, especially as the force now on the island was equally obviously inadequate. The paratroops had been withdrawn, and all that was left to guard an island with a coastline fifty miles long—much of it consisting of flat, sandy beaches—were the four rifle companies of infantry and 234 men from the RAF Regiment—a total force of 1,600 men including noncombatants—plus some 4,000 infantry and artillerymen from the original Italian garrison.

Early on the morning of October 1, a German convoy of seven transports, seven landing craft, and several caiques, all escorted by three destroyers and some E-boats, was reported off Naxos, so three Hunt-class destroyers were immediately dispatched from Alexandria to intercept and destroy. As the convoy was reported to have left the Piraeus, it was assumed that it bore reinforcement troops for Rhodes (upon which were already stationed the crack assault division that Middle East headquarters believed would undertake any invasion duties), so the British destroyers patrolled first in the Scarpanto Straits during the night of October 1-2, then during the dangerous daylight hours in the waters to the southeast of Rhodes itself.

By the evening of October 2 they had seen nothing of the convoy, but they were running short of fuel, so concluding that their intended prey had turned west and gone to Crete instead, they returned to Alexandria. In normal circumstances, their place would have been taken by fleet destroyers of the Eighth Flotilla, but it had been decided that these should act as escorts to the battleships *King George V* and

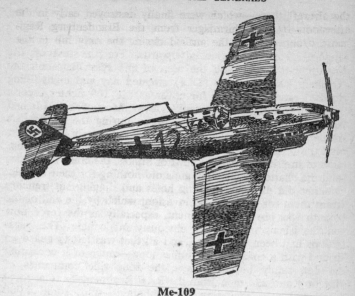

Me-109

Howe, which had arrived in Alexandria after duties off Sicily and were now required at home. So for the moment, the waters of the Aegean were free of all Royal Navy presence except for some small craft operating close along the Turkish coast running supplies into Leros and Samos, and three submarines on routine patrol who saw nothing of the convoy.

Kampfgruppe Mueller arrived off the landing beaches of Cos before dawn on October 3, and by five o'clock a battalion of the sixty-fifth Panzer Grenadier Regiment was ashore between Marmari and Lambia, and one from the Sixteenth Panzer grenadiers was ashore near Cape Foça. Both battalions were supported by assault engineer detachments, and the one on the west coast by a battery of self-propelled guns from the Twenty-second Artillery Regiment. As they moved purposefully inland, Junkers 88s and Me 109s appeared over the island, and a bombardment of Antimachia airfield, Cos town, and Marmari began, which was to last all day. Within half an hour of landing, men of the Sixty-fifth Panzer Grenadiers had found and destroyed ten Spitfires camouflaged near Marmari, while at Antimachia the Stuka attacks were holding down all the aircraft there—which were finally destroyed early in the afternoon by Fallschirmjäger from the Brandenburg Regiment, dropped on to the airfield during the only lull in the bombing. These then quickly wiped out the few survivors of D Compay of the DLIs and the RAF Bofors gunners who remained, and the last airfield in the Aegean was lost to the British.

In the morning assault pioneers from the 999th Regiment with a battery of mountain guns had come ashore in Kamara Bay, quickly silenced the Italian artillery in the area and then moved up toward the center of the island, driving Italian units and British survivors up into the area where the Fallschirmjäger and Panzer grenadiers were now closing in on Cos town. By late afternoon the battle had risen to a peak of concentrated violence in the northern end of the island that had rarely been surpassed in the experience of anyone there —British, Italian or German. Mortar bombs, light and medium artillery shells, small arms fire, and all the time the screaming Stuka bombs rained on the dwindling band of defenders, sheltering at first behind ramshackle stone walls (the ground was far too hard to dig trenches) and then between the buildings as they were forced back into Cos itself.

With the last Italian artillery posts overrun and the perimeter back to the Cos outskirts, the DLI's commanding officer called a hurried conference of the remaining company commanders to decide how to get the rest of the men out, and with the bad luck that had dogged his battalion for so long, a mortar bomb exploded among them, killing one and badly wounding the rest.

By midnight the Germans controlled all of Cos except the dock area, and upon this they focused searchlights, sniping and bombing everything that moved. Small parties of British and Italian soldiers sneaked their way out of the town to climb the hills and make for a rendezvous at Cardamena, with the admirable intention of carrying out their last orders, which were to try to continue the fight in guerrilla fashion. But most of them were rounded up after a few days, despite enterprising attempts to escape to Turkey or to the other islands by rowboat, salvaged caique, or raft, a few of which were successful.

During the next two or three weeks, caiques manned by SBS men crept into the dark bays by night and picked up over a hundred hungry and bedraggled survivors, but organized resistance to the Germans on Cos had been over by the morning of October 4, and the diary of the Oberkommando der Wehrmacht could curtly record:

Cos occupied. 600 English prisoners and 2,500 Italian. Forty guns and twenty-two partly destroyed aircraft captured.

The fighting had been almost Thermopylaen in intensity, and what the diary does not record is the fate of the Italian officers who had been captured. On the mornings of October 4, 5, and 6, ninety of them, including the garrison commander, had been taken down on to the beach and shot. Generalleutnant Friedrich Mueller was building a reputation for efficiency and ruthlessness, which by the end of the war would make him one of the most feared men in the Mediterranean.

Mr. Churchill's involvement in all this had been, of course, one of baffled hope. Like Sir Alan Brooke he had been forced to accept the cancellation of the stand-still order and watch with sorrow the departure of the landing craft to the Indian Ocean. By the time the short armistice was signed on September 3, he was back in Washington, and both prime minister and president were concentrating on the British and American invasions of the Italian mainland, and both were also much concerned with a speech Mr. Churchill was to make at Harvard on Anglo-American amity.

It was not until his return to the United Kingdom on September 19 that he was able to turn much of his attention to matters in the Aegean, but on September 22 he received from General Wilson a report upon the intentions to "carry out piratical war on enemy communications" there, and also a suggestion that as the Tenth Indian Division had now become available for operations, it might be worth considering another descent on the only island from which domination of the area could be assured—Rhodes. An armored brigade and a parachute battalion were still available; as before; what was missing was transport, of which the minimum requirements would be three LSTs, a hospital ship, which could also act as headquarters, ships to carry vehicles, naval escorts, and enough aircraft to lift the paratroops.

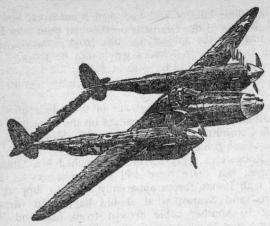

Lockheed P-38 Lightning

On September 25, Mr. Churchill cabled General Eisenhower the details of these requirements and two days later was delighted to receive a reply stating that Eisenhower was sure that they could be met—and it was obvious that they could be from the immense arsenal now accumulating. That this was the case with the supreme commander became even more evident when news of the invasion of Cos reached him, for he immediately released six squadrons of Lightnings, and for five days following the fall of the island, they dominated the air above the Aegean and seriously worried General-leutnant Mueller and his command.

Then news of their use in the area reached Washington. A curt order from the Combined Chiefs of Staff arrived in Algiers, and General Eisenhower ordered their withdrawal. Very shortly afterward, a cable arrived in London from him to the effect that he and the commanders in chief—Alexander, Tedder, and Cunningham—had reluctantly come to the conclusion that the moment for success in the Aegean had passed and that all available strength in the Mediterranean should henceforth be committed to Italy.

In something approaching despair, Churchill sent a long cable to Mr. Roosevelt, begging him to order the release of what were truly miniscule requirements for only a limited period. But Mr. Roosevelt showed the cable to General

Marshall, and the reply was as near a plain rebuff as ever passed between the two men. Two more cables passed between them on the subject, the one from Roosevelt arguing that an expedition to Rhodes would not be the end of the affair and that it would have to be followed up by more and more troops sent to more and more islands—and where would it all end?

In the Balkans was the answer in the minds of General Marshall and many of his colleagues on the American Chiefs of Staff Committee, and certainly in Mr. Stimson's. . . . And this they were firmly determined to resist.

Mr. Roosevelt's reply therefore quenched Mr. Churchill's last hopes; but there were still large numbers of British troops, with Italian forces apparently eager to support them, on Leros and Samos; what should happen to them? On October 10 another cable arrived from Maitland Wilson suggesting that their evacuation would be a matter of considerable difficulty, that their retention in the area not an impossibility given Turkish aid or at least connivance, and their continued presence an irritation to the enemy, which would cause them to divert and hold forces in the area that might otherwise be available in France or in Russia.

The reply went off at once:

Prime Minister to General Wilson 10 Oct 43

Cling on if you possibly can. It will be a splendid achievement. Talk it over with Eden and see what help you can get from the Turk. If after everything has been done you are forced to quit I will support you, but victory is the prize.

Evidently, the lessons of the Norwegian campaign, of Crete, of Malta—even of the loss of the *Repulse* and the *Prince of Wales*—had not yet been learned, and this decision for which Mr. Churchill and General Maitland Wilson must share responsibility (and Sir Alan Brooke in the absence of any strong protest from him) was one of the more unfortunate in the history of the Second World War. It should have become quite obvious by this time that isolated garrisons cannot endure in the face of enemy hostility unless they have effective control of the air—not only above their own location but also above their supply lines. And Generalleutnant

Mueller was not the man to put up with "irritation" for a moment longer than he had to.

The Royal Navy was the first to feel the shock of his hostility. Two destroyers had already been lost on the Leros run before Cos had fallen, and now with the last British airstrip gone the losses mounted. Two cruisers were damaged and a destroyer sunk in the Scarpanto Straits on October 9. By the end of the month two more cruisers and two more destroyers had been put out of action and another two destroyers sunk, one carrying two rifle companies and the headquarter company of the Royal East Kents (the Buffs), who thereby lost six officers and 136 non-commissioned officers and men, in addition to the naval casualties.

Many years afterward, one of the cruiser captains told the author that these losses in what he called "the most pointless campaign of the war" brought him and his fellow commanders nearer to mutiny than any other situation during their naval careers, and only the plight of the unfortunate soldiers on Leros took them back into such dangerous areas again! Orders from above, he said, would not have been enough.

As for the defenders of the two islands, there were three British battalions on Leros—Fourth Battalion Royal East Kents, Second Battalion the Royal Irish Fusiliers, and the First Battalion the King's Own Royal Regiment—some five thousand Italian garrison troops of whom only the artillery (manning nearly a hundred elderly and poorly emplaced guns) were likely to prove reliable, and at the end some fifty assorted LRDG and SBS men who had been given a roving commission to deal with any Fallshirmjäger—whose presence was not expected as the island was deemed too rocky and mountainous for paratroops to be landed.

On Samos were the Second Battalion of the Royal West Kent Regiment and some 350 men of the Greek Sacred Squadron (200 of whom had been parachuted in, such was their eagerness to be involved in the battle to come), but it was not expected that Samos would be attacked at least until Leros had fallen.

All through the second half of October the bombing of Leros had been steadily increasing. Dorniers were now joining in from the Greek mainland, but mostly it was Stukas, given now a new lease of life for almost the first time since the campaign in France, while above and around them flew

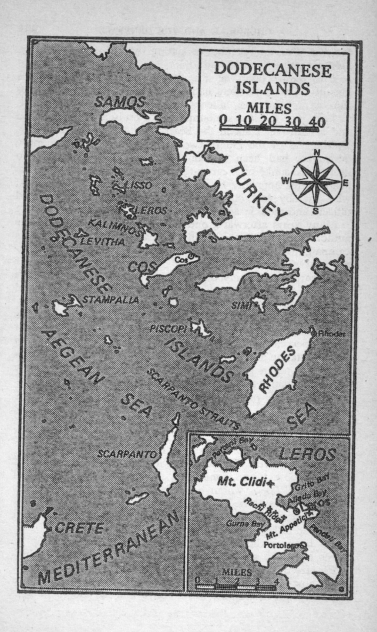

DODECANESE ISLANDS

MILES
0 10 20 30 40

SAMOS

TURKEY

N
W   E
S

DODECANESE

LISSO

LEROS

KALIMNOS

LEVITHA

COS

Cos

STAMPALIA

SIMI

PISCOPI

ISLANDS

Rhodes

AEGEAN

RHODES

SEA

SCARPANTO STRAITS

SEA

SCARPANTO

LEROS

Pergini Bay

Mt. Clidi

Grifo Bay

Alinda Bay

Rachi Ridge

LEROS

Gurna Bay

Mt. Appetici

Portolago

Portolago

Vendici Bay

CRETE

MEDITERRANEAN

MILES
0   1   2   3   4

the Me 109s, completely outclassing the pitifully new Beau-fighters and Mitchells that put in occasional appearances, only to remain in the area for twenty minutes or so as they had to return to Cyprus or even North Africa. And as November began, the intensity of air attack grew.

Bristol Beaufighter

In the meantime, Mueller had been clearing his flanks. Simi, after a brilliantly conducted defense on October 7, had been evacuated a week later in the face of what would obviously have been an overwhelming second attack. Stam-palia was captured on October 22 from a platoon of the Royal Irish Rifles. On October 27–28 the battle of Levitha had been fought, in which the Long-range Desert Group suffered the greatest losses of their career. And by November 10, Mueller had assembled a striking force large enough to undertake the main task, the shipping to transport them, and sufficient aircraft to give them complete cover.

The invasion force was sighted early on the morning of November 12 and immediately engaged by the Italian coastal batteries, which drove off the force approaching Gurna Bay despite the inevitable Stuka waves that promptly arrived to put the battery out of action. At the northern end of the island, however, the Germans were using smaller landing craft, and these dodged the shells from the coastal battery there and put the majority of their assault troops ashore. With admirable enterprise and efficiency, the troops pro-ceeded to haul themselves up the precipitous sides of Mount

Clidi, the commanding feature of the area, which both Brigadier Tilney, the British fortress commander, and his predecessor had deemed unclimbable and thus had not bothered greatly with its defense.

That this was not the only miscalculation the command had made was demonstrated at noon when a flock of Ju 52 transport planes arrived and promptly disgorged some six hundred parachutists. Although their landing casualties were undoubtedly high and those that reached the ground unharmed were then cut off from their supply containers by SBS snipers, there were still enough of them to take almost complete control of the narrow waist of the island between Gurna and Alinda Bays.

By mid-afternoon, another sea-borne force had come ashore south of Alinda Bay practically unopposed, as the Italian garrison troops there seem to have regarded themselves as noncombatant. So German forces were now pushing inland on each side of Leros, against defenses already overstretched and only too conscious that not only were there enemy parachutists somewhere behind them, but that Stukas would arrive overhead within minutes of their opening fire on the invaders. One company of the Royal Irish Fusiliers managed to fling back the first German attacks on Mount Appetici, but their losses through bombing and machine-gun fire as they advanced across the open, rocky ground were so great that the men of the Brandenburg Regiment—Mueller's shock troops—had no difficulty from then on in holding a narrow strip of coastline onto which more and more of their compatriots could flood ashore.

This episode illuminated yet another crucial aspect of the situation on Leros. Except for limited help from Samos, the British on Leros when the battle opened were on their own, but the Germans could be, and were, continually reinforced as the battle progressed. On the morning of November 13 this was demonstrated yet again when schoonerload after schoonerload of the Brandenburg Regiment came ashore at both Grifo Bay and Pandeli Bay, while shortly after dawn another formation of Ju 52s arrived to release yet another two hundred Fallschirmjäger.

These, however, met with even more misfortune than their comrades the day before. A minor gale was blowing, and many of those not killed or hurt when they hit the ground were dragged by their parachutes across the rocks and low

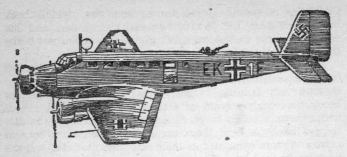

Junkers Ju 52

walls while frantically trying to release the harness clips, with often disastrous results. At least two of the transports were hit, wobbled out of formation lower and lower over the sea, their cargoes at last jumping clear but the majority drowning, their bodies floating for hours beneath canopies spread like water lilies on the Aegean sea.

But those who did land safely joined their comrades in what has been described as "splendid isolation" at the top of Rachi Ridge, and although the SBS and LRDG men thought that they were scoring at least a partial victory in keeping them there, the awkward fact was that the German parachutists blocked all communication between fortress headquarters and the north of the island in which most of the fighting was taking place. Thus all attempts during that day to dislodge the Germans from their dominant position on Mount Clidi failed because nothing could be done to coordinate attacks from both sides at once.

Yet during that second day of the battle, it seemed to the British troops that they were holding their own. Their casualties had been heavy but so had been those of their opponents. And during the morning there was an episode that spectacularly demonstrated that German mastery of warfare was not without lapse. One of their landing barges loaded with ammunition nosed its way into Alinda Bay under the impression that it was in friendly hands and was promptly blown apart by Bofors guns and an Italian battery; and later an Arado seaplane made the same mistake and was promptly riddled with machine-gun fire.

But this success brought—as did all the defenders' successes—an inevitable riposte, and by noon the Italian battery had been bombed out of existence, and by that evening there were only three Bofors guns left in action, these constituting the island's sole antiaircraft defense.

The pattern for the next two days was a repeat of the first two except that no more attempts were made to drop parachutists. But landing barges, Seibel ferries, and caiques brought a steady stream of German reinforcements ashore under Messerschmidt cover, Stukas bombed strongpoints that seemed likely to hold them up, and the defenders became more and more exhausted as their casualties mounted and the tasks facing the remainder became ever more onerous. On the night of November 14–15, some relief was provided when nearly two companies of the Royal West Kents were precariously brought across from Samos, and in the late evening of the 15th, most of the rest of the battalion arrived—to find that their comrades of A and C Company had been fed piecemeal into the developing battle and practically wiped out!

By the morning of November 16, there were signs of the danse macabre of defeat among the British formations. Signals did not get through; patrols sent out on reconnaissance missions failed to return, while those on offensive missions were wiped out almost to a man; companies gathered themselves wearily together to storm a position and found it unoccupied, so they relinquished it, only to be ordered to take it again and find it strongly held.

The battle in fact had reached a stage often seen on the sports field, when nothing the losing side attempts goes right, while the winners can take the most adventurous risks and succeed. During the afternoon, Brigadier Tilney found himself engaged in vicious hand-to-hand fighting around the headquarter's cave, seven of his staff officers were killed, and he himself was taken prisoner. By 5:30 P.M. the swastika was waving above the fortress headquarters, and he formally surrendered the island.

The news, as so often in such circumstances, took quite a long time to circulate, and sporadic fighting went on until after dark. But by then the survivors were split up into small groups all over the island and were so tired that when the firing died away, they could do nothing but lie down and sleep. And the next morning the majority of them were taken prisoner.

Only the remaining SBS and LRDG men (who had lost

their revered commanding officer, Lieutenant-Colonel "Jake" Easonsmith) quickly organized their escape. Major Jellicoe, who had been in fortress headquarters when Tilney announced the surrender, bluffed his way past the encircling Germans to rejoin his men, and by the early hours of November 17 they were all aboard a captured Italian caique making for the nearby island of Lisso. There they remained all day before making for their own base, hidden discreetly in Turkish waters; but of the four infantry battalions who had fought on Leros, less than two hundred and fifty survivors got away.

During the following two nights, Samos was evacuated. The staffs, the British and Greek forces, the Italian commander, and the metropolitan archbishop, all dressed in somewhat outré civilian garb, left in a fleet of caiques and landed in Turkey. When on November 20 it was discovered that the Germans had still not landed on Samos, a second caique squadron went in to bring out another fourteen hundred soldiers and civilians in one night, and nearly three thousand the next. Turkish trains eventually transported most of them down into Syria, and when eventually Generalleutnant Mueller announced the island's occupation, he claimed only 2,500 Italian soldiers taken prisoner and a few guns.

And as on Cos and Leros, the Italian officers taken prisoner were shot, thus paying the highest price for British folly.

CHAPTER TWELVE

The campaign in the Dodecanese was the last series of Second World War battles in which Britain attempted to play an independent role. Whether the tactical lessons regarding the necessity of air cover were learned or not (and they certainly were in the purely military circles) the strategic lesson sank in deeply. Britain was no longer paying the piper and henceforth, she must dance to the tune of those who were. Mr. Churchill's Middle East strategy in the First World War had been defeated by military incompetence, and in the Second by lack of understanding, lack of sympathy, and, one suspects, a determination in one narrow corner to show who was master.

From 1943 onward, Britain's role in the defeat of Germany was secondary at best, and as President Roosevelt's unfortunate belief in M. Stalin's political beneficence grew, Mr. Churchill's influence in the topmost circles of power diminished. At the Cairo Conferences at the end of 1943, even Chiang Kai-Shek seemed to hold more of the president's regard than the prime minister, while at Yalta the leaders of the two great powers—one an idealist and the other a cynic—laid the foundations of the world in which we live without paying much more than polite attention to the leader of the country that had fought the common enemy longer than they had.

As far as the prosecution of the war against Germany was concerned, by the end of 1943 all attention was concentrated on the buildup to Operation Overlord—the massing of huge armies in southern Britain and the nightly dispatch of huge fleets of bombers over Europe. Events in the Mediterranean occupied a secondary place in the world's attention, much to the irritation of those who remained in the theater, for the fighting in Italy was as grim and demanding as any in the war. Despite Sir Alan Brooke's disappointment at what he felt was his failure to persuade the Americans of the value of his Mediterranean policy, it was nevertheless not totally ineffective; in July 1943 there had been eighteen German divisions in Italy and the Balkans, but by the end of the year there were forty-nine.

Mr. Churchill's relations with the generals had now undergone a major change. For one thing, the supreme commander of the gigantic operation about to be launched from the shores of Britain was an American over whom, in the last resort, Mr. Churchill had no control. As it happened, General Eisenhower was a man of immense charm and understanding, and his personal relations with Mr. Churchill were as close and friendly as those with the British generals, and in the case of General Montgomery perhaps even better.

The most important reason for the changed relationship, though, was that now there was a winning team. Even had Mr. Churchill still retained the authority to appoint and dismiss the top commanders, he would have had no need to exercise it, for the days of retreat and military disaster were over. It was not true as Mr. Churchill is reputed to have said, that "before Alamein we never had a victory, after Alamein we never had a defeat"—witness the O'Connor Offensive and the Dodecanese campaign—but there is sufficient truth in it for it to be obvious why the constant harrying, almost bullying, to which Wavell and Auchinleck had been subjected, ceased after the advance across North Africa.

Of course Mr. Churchill was much concerned with the details of Operation Overlord but far more with matters of manpower and equipment than of tactics or even of timing. He visited barracks and airfields, watched training exercises, inspected factories, and talked to the men and women turning out the guns, the vehicles, the aircraft, the shells. In particular he was interested in the "mulberries"—the huge artificial harbors to be towed across the Channel and through which all the supplies and reinforcements for the initial stages of the battle would pass.

Matters of strategy and tactics, however, were now left to those in whose profession they lay. Except for a minor difference of opinion between Mr. Churchill and General Montgomery about the proportion of vehicles to fighting men in the first waves of Operation Overlord, there was little except congratulations to all concerned when the prime minister spoke at a huge briefing conference held at St. Paul's School in West London on May 15, just three weeks before D-day. His Majesty King George VI was also present, as were the British Chiefs of Staff, Field Marshal Smuts, and the main army and navy commanders.

It was an impressive but sobering occasion. The next three weeks were a time of some tension. Mr. Churchill's wish to be present on the beaches during the prelanding bombardment was eventually thwarted by a personal appeal from the king, who pointed out that he was both younger than Churchill, a sailor by training, and head of the armed services, yet he had yielded to pressure and agreed to stay at home. And he did not wish to face the immediate future without Mr. Churchill's advice and guidance. Reluctantly Mr. Churchill acceded to the royal request, though he continued rather grumpily to complain about it for the rest of his life.

It was not, of course, possible to keep him out of France once the Anglo-American armies had formed a bridgehead, however small, and accompanied by Field Marshal Smuts and Sir Alan Brooke, he visited Montgomery in his headquarters château on June 10, only four days after the landings. The line of advance was only three miles away, and not continuous, but his sense of adventure was not satisfied until he had persuaded Admiral Vian to allow the destroyer on which they were all traveling back to England to take part in a bombardment of enemy-held shores by battleships and cruisers—for which, of course, the destroyer had to go far closer in than the ships with heavier armament.

"I had a jolly day on Monday on the beaches and inland," he began his account written two days later to Mr. Roosevelt, ending, "How I wish you were here!"

He visited France on several occasions during the following months, though perhaps the most exciting was in March 1945 when the Allied armies had closed up to the Rhine and the First U.S. Army had captured the Remagen Bridge almost undamaged. Mr. Churchill accompanied by his private secretary and police attendant arrived at Montgomery's headquarters soon afterward, and during a tour of the front with General Eisenhower, gazed across four hundred yards of flat water into Germany itself. The supreme commander had shortly to depart on other business, but Mr. Churchill had seen a small launch nearby, and somewhat to his surprise Montgomery agreed to his suggestion that they cross and "have a look at the other side." They landed in brilliant sunshine and spent half an hour on the enemy shore without hindrance or the slightest sign of warlike activity.

Nevertheless Mr. Churchill managed to find himself under fire a little later while the party was examining the wreck of the railway bridge at Wesel; so he did not consider the trip an entire waste of time.

There was not much more of the war in Europe left to fight. Mr. Churchill suffered a deep personal loss when Mr. Roosevelt died suddenly on April 12, but even this blow was smothered in the tide of great events flowing at the time, for the Anglo-American armies were driving deep into Germany; on April 25 American and Russian forces met at Torgau on the Elbe; and eighteen days after the death of the American president, Hitler committed suicide in the bunker in Berlin. A man of demonic genius, who had taken his country in twelve years from poverty to immense power and then back into disaster, had gone, and the world could set about the task of repairing the damage he had caused.

At midnight on May 8, 1945, hostilities in Europe ended with the unconditional surrender of the German armed forces, and the following afternoon, Mr. Churchill delivered the last of his wartime speeches to the nation. It was not the paean of praise and hope that many of his listeners expected, for the deliberations at Yalta had disabused Mr. Churchill of any hopes he may have had of Russian goodwill toward—or even tolerance of—political systems other than their own, and already developments in the "liberated" countries of eastern Europe had confirmed his worst suspicions. After warnings of the need for even further effort and indeed sacrifice, he pointed out that there would not have been much point in destroying the Nazi régime and its philosophy if its place was to be taken by an equally tyrannous system that would deliberately distort the words freedom, democracy and liberation from their true meanings. But the end of the speech was a reminder of the old, true Churchillian rhetoric.

"I told you hard things at the beginning of these last five years; you did not shrink, and I should be unworthy of your confidence and generosity if I did not still cry: Forward, unflinching, unswerving, indomitable, till the whole task is done and the whole world safe and clean. Advance Britannia!"

* * *

Because of the outbreak of war in September 1939 and the necessity since then for concentrating the nation's mind on beating the enemy, there had not been a general election in Britain since the end of 1935. There had been occasions during the war against Germany when some of Mr. Churchill's critics maintained that this was a palpable breach of the constitution, but such complaints were brushed aside not only by the sweep of events but also by the huge majorities by which he and his government won the votes of confidence whenever matters were put to the test.

But with the defeat of Germany, Mr. Churchill decided that the time had come for the country to be given an opportunity either to confirm or to end his authority as prime minister. He almost certainly believed that his own personal popularity would be enough to ensure a sweeping victory for the Conservative Party of which he was leader, and was thus astounded when they were swept from power and, to use his own words, ". . . all our enemies having surrendered unconditionally or being about to do so, I was immediately dismissed by the British electorate from all further conduct of their affairs."

One can appreciate the reasons for the bitterness underlying the words. The shock to his personal esteem must have been traumatic. What has always been a matter of some argument were the reasons for so overwhelming a defeat. Lord Beaverbrook's political campaign on behalf of the Conservative Party has been blamed, the Conservatives themselves have charged that while they were devoting all their energies between 1939 and 1945 to winning the war, the Labour Party under Mr. Attlee were concentrating on Socialist propaganda and influencing the minds of the electorate by almost subliminal means, especially the younger ones who had not voted before.

If, as has been claimed, it was the "Services Vote" that swept Mr. Churchill out of office, there could be another reason that has not yet been aired—political naiveté, amounting in many cases to ignorance.

In 1935 the qualifying age for voting in a general election was twenty-one, which meant that to have taken an intelligent interest in that election one must be at least thirty-one in 1945—and the vast majority of the men and women serving in Britain's forces at that time were younger than that, and their recent activities had given them little opportunity to concern themselves with purely political matters. Moreover, politicians in those days were no more popular than they are today with the British public, the majority of whom are bleakly uninterested in anything unconnected with their personal professions or hobbies; all we knew was that we had been separated from our families for many years, we had suffered pain, exhaustion, hunger, acute discomfort, and bursts of paralyzing fear, seen our friends killed in horrifying circumstances, and often heard by post of the deaths of brothers, fathers, sisters, and mothers.

This set of circumstances had been brought about by the leaders of the nations, not by the people themselves who never want war, but by those who by one method or another have risen to power: by politicians. And between the wars and especially during the years immediately preceding its outbreak, Conservatives had been the politicians in power for most of the time.

So away with them!

And a surprisingly large number of us, including author, were as astonished as Mr. Churchill when we discovered that we had throw him out, too! Surely Mr. Churchill was above party politics, we felt. Vaguely, too, we knew that in the years before the war he had been very unpopular with the Conservatives, and to a small extent we had felt that in kicking them out we were teaching them a lesson for not listening to him when he and they might have prevented the holocaust through which we had just passed.

When we found out what we had done, we rationalized it in several doubtful ways. It was time he retired, we told ourselves. And in any case, the king would obviously now make him a peer of the realm . . . a viscount, an earl, perhaps even a duke to follow in the tradition of Wellington or even his own great ancestor, Marlborough. Surely he would not remain just Mr. Winston Churchill, leader of His Majesty's Opposition?

But we did not understand the springs of his ambition, the main joy and excitement of his life, which was the cut and thrust of parliamentary debate. Not wanting to have anything at all to do with parliamentary life ourselves, we could not believe that he was so different from us; and so for six years he and his party were out of office, not returning until 1951.

By that time, however, the country as a whole and the ex-servicemen who may or may not have been responsible for his dismissal in 1945, had had ample opportunity to assure him of their continued affection and respect. It was Monty—Field Marshal Viscount Montgomery of Alamein—who found the words, indeed the accolade. In the Albert Hall in London, at the first Africa Star reunion at which everybody who had served in the desert and who could get there was present, he introduced that familiar, short, dark-coated bull-dog figure—to deafening cheers and applause that went on for minutes—as what we all felt him to be:

The Greatest Living Englishman.

Nothing happened while he lived to make us change our minds, and since his death that is what he has remained in our memories.

NOTES TO SOURCES

Chapter 1 Débâcle in France
1 Winston S. Churchill, *The Second World War*, II, Houghton Mifflin, 1949, p. 24.
2 Ibid., pp. 103–4.
3 Quoted by Arthur Bryant, *The Alanbrooke War Diaries 1939–43: The Turn of the Tide*, Fontana, 1957, p. 143.
Chapter 2 The Battle of Britain
1 Winston S. Churchill, op. cit., pp. 198–9.
Chapter 3 Wavell's 30,000
1 Quoted by John Connell, *Wavell, Scholar and Soldier*, Collins, 1964, pp. 255–6.
2 Quoted by Kenneth Macksey, *Armoured Crusader*, Hutchinson, 1967, pp. 111–12, by permission of Mrs. G. Tasker.
Chapter 4 Wavell's Eclipse
1 Quoted by Major-General I.S.O. Playfair *et al.*, *History of the Second World War, The Mediterranean and the Middle East*, II, H.M.S.O., 1956, p. 203.
2 Quoted by John Connell, op. cit., pp. 434–5.
Chapter 5 Barbarossa and Pearl Harbour
1 Winston S. Churchill, op. cit., III, Houghton Mifflin, pp. 332–3.
2 Quoted by John Connell, *Auchinleck*, Cassell, 1959, pp. 267–8.
3 Ibid., p. 268.
4 Quoted by Arthur Bryant, op. cit., p. 217.
5 Quoted by John Connell, op. cit., p. 336.
6 Major-General Sir Howard Kippenberger, *Infantry Brigadier*, Oxford University Press, 1949, p. 81.
7 Winston S. Churchill, op. cit., II, p. 539.

8 Lord Moran, *Churchill, The Struggle for Survival 1940–65*, Houghton Mifflin, 1966, p. 9.
9 Ibid., pp. 16–17.

Chapter 6   Disaster in the Desert
  1 Quoted by John Connell, op. cit., p. 423.
  2 Winston S. Churchill, op. cit., IV, 1951, p. 21.
  3 Major-General F.W. von Mellenthin, *Panzer Battles: A Study of the Employment of Armor in the Second World War*, Ballantine Books (N.Y.), 1971, pp. 104–5, copyright 1956 by the University of Oklahoma Press.
  4 Winston S. Churchill, op. cit., IV, p. 261.
  5 Quoted by John Connell, op. cit., p. 500.
  6 B.H. Liddell Hart (ed.), *The Rommel Papers*, Collins, 1953, p. 208.

Chapter 7   The Winning Team
  1 Lord Tedder, *With Prejudice*, Little, Brown, 1966, p. 313.
  2 Major-General Francis de Guingand, *Operation Victory*, Hodder and Stoughton, 1947, p. 136.
  3 Quoted by Arthur Bryant, op. cit., p. 394.

Chapter 8   The Critical Months
  1 Quoted by Arthur Bryant, op. cit., p. 591.
  2 Ibid., p. 420.
  3 Winston S. Churchill, op. cit., IV, pp. 537–8.
  4 Ibid., p. 539.

Chapter 9   Victory in North Africa
  1 Winston S. Churchill, op. cit., IV, p. 488.
  2 Quoted by Arthur Bryant, op. cit., p. 473.

Chapter 10   Italy and the Allies
  1 Quoted by Michael Howard, *History of the Second World War Grand Startegy*, IV, HMSO, 1972, p. 432 (C.C.S. 237/1).
  2 Ibid., p. 561 (Stimpson's Report: Matloff p. 214).

Chapter 11   The Aegean Venture
  1 Winston S. Churchill, op. cit., V, 1952, p. 193.

Epilogue
  1 Winston S. Churchill, op. cit., VI, 1954, p. 479.
  2 Ibid, I, p. 526.

ABOUT THE AUTHOR

BARRIE PITT was born in 1918. The son of a naval officer, he spent his childhood in service circles in naval ports. He joined the Army in 1939 and served in the European and Middle East theatres. In 1962 he published "1918—THE LAST ACT," which brought considerable success and an invitation to join the production team of the BBC Television series "The Great War." After that he was commissioned to assemble and edit the enormous "History of the Second World War." He then became the editor-in-chief for Ballantine's Illustrated History of World War II, which sold nearly 20 million copies throughout the world.

JACK LE VIEN is an American film and television director and producer living in London. While in the U.S. Army he met Churchill during the campaigns in North Africa and Europe. After the war, he became News Editor of Pathe News and later an independent filmmaker. Among his various films, TV series and Specials are a number based on Sir Winston's writings, made under the provisions of several agreements with the former Prime Minister. He is a Colonel in the U.S. Army Reserve and is also President of TCA, Travel Corporation of America.